STRONG MOTHERS

A Resource for Mothers and Carers of Children who have been Sexually Assaulted

Anne Peake and Marion Fletcher

STRONG MOTHERS: A RESOURCE FOR MOTHERS AND CARERS OF CHILDREN WHO HAVE BEEN SEXUALLY ASSAULTED

Russell House Publishing Limited

First published in 1997 by:
Russell House Publishing Limited
4 St. George's House
The Business Park
Uplyme Road
Lyme Regis
Dorset DT7 3LS

British Library Cataloguing-in-Publication Data:
A catalogue record for this manual is available from the British Library.

ISBN: 1-898924-04-X

Text design and layout by: Jeremy Spencer, London

Printed by: Ashford Press, Southampton.

Contents

When a woman is told or realises that her child has been sexually assaulted by her partner or someone she knew and trusted; the thing she never thought would happen to her and one of the worst things that could ever happen, has happened. Nothing will ever be the same again; not her child, her family, her faith in people, her life, her hopes for the future: nothing will be the same. The danger is that mothers feel that their children, families, and lives, have been ruined by what has happened.

This book has been designed so that it can be read as a whole or used in sections as and when they seem relevant and useful. For this reason there is some repetition. We have included the words of mothers of abused children, as we are sure they are the clearest words of all. They are in frames so they can be picked out with ease.

For mothers of children who have been sexually assaulted

The book has been written by mothers for mothers of children who have been sexually assaulted by someone they know. Our message is that you can walk on. The path will not always be clear and signposted, there will be steep mountains to climb and you may be buffeted by bad weather, as you carry your family or what is left of your family. The only way is to walk. We hope you can read this as you journey and that it helps you to think about what has happened and to know you are not alone. The book makes suggestions but has no answers because we believe you know yourself and your children, and you know where you are going. Travel one day at a time. Rest when you can, and see sunny days for what they are. You will arrive at a place far from where you set off, feeling more and knowing more. We wish you strength.

For others doing the caring

The authors recognise it isn't always the mother of a sexually abused child who is subsequently the main care giver. It can be non-abusing fathers, step-parents, grandparents, relatives, foster carers and adoptive parents. If you are the main care giver of a child who has been sexually abused, this book will offer the support and information you are seeking.

For caring professionals

This book has been written by mothers for mothers. It is also an invaluable resource for professionals, including: social workers, child protection officers, doctors, health visitors, teachers, police officers and solicitors, any professional working with people whose lives have been affected by sexual abuse.

This book gives the professional who is often caught up in the management of procedures, the opportunity to view the situation from the mother's perspective.

If you know someone who might want to read this book...

Information on how you can buy a copy is provided over the page.

If you want to tell someone about this book

Please photocopy this page and the form opposite and give it to them.

Strong mothers: A Resource for Mothers and Carers of Children who have been Sexually Assaulted has been written jointly by Marion Fletcher, a mother whose children have been sexually assaulted, and Anne Peake, a Principal Psychologist with Oxfordshire Social Services. This unique resource will:

- help **mothers whose children have been sexually assaulted** to learn to live with the feeling that "nothing will be the same again"; help them to realise that they are not alone in their journey by including, wherever possible, the views of other mothers of sexually abused children in their own words; and give sound advice and information on what to expect in terms of support, the law and carrying the emotional burden.

- provide to **other caregivers of sexually abused children** – non-abusing fathers, step-parents, grandparents, relatives, foster carers and adoptive parents – the support and information they are seeking.

- enable professionals – **social workers, doctors, teachers, solicitors and the police**, for whom it is all too easy to be caught up in the management of procedures – to view what they are trying to achieve from the mother's perspective.

Contents: Introduction. What is child sexual abuse? Why didn't my child tell me she/he was being sexually abused? Why didn't I know? What happens when a child tells? And then what? Help for your child. The prevention of sexual abuse. Your journey. Useful reading. A4 paperback 96 pages. 1-898924-04-X. Available now.

How to obtain this book

It is the goal of the authors to offer help to mothers and carers of children who have been sexually assaulted. A central part of this goal is to make Strong Mothers available as easily as possible to people who may not want themselves or their children to be identified. Here are details of how to order the book. Please choose the one that you are most comfortable with.

• From bookshops

Take a copy of the order form to almost any bookshop and ask them to order it for you. The information they need is on the form. If you do not wish to be identified, ask a friend to do this for you.

• From Russell House Publishing

Read the next paragraph carefully. Then complete the order form and send it to us with your cheque.

If you do not wish to receive any subsequent mail from Russell House Publishing or anyone else, please make sure you tick the relevant box on the order form. But please bear in mind that publishers are human and sometimes make mistakes, like anyone else. If you want an absolute guarantee that your name is kept 100% confidential, ask a good friend to send the order form on your behalf and have them write the cheque for you as well.

| **OUR FREE TRIAL GUARANTEE:** | You may return any item ordered below in clean and resaleable condition for a full refund up to 30 days after it is sent to you. Please include a copy of the invoice. |

✔ Please supply the following items:

_____ copies of **Strong Mothers** (ISBN 1-898924-04-X) £14.95 each _____

Add postage and packing (**UK**) £1.50 <u>per item</u> (**Elsewhere**) £2.50 <u>per item</u>.   **PLUS P&P**
PAYMENT: Individual customers: please pay in advance.   **Total (incl p&p)**

❑ I enclose a cheque made payable to **Russell House Publishing Ltd.**
❑ Please send an invoice and my purchases to my organisation for payment on receipt.

IN A RUSH? QUESTIONS? Please fax or phone: we will respond by return.

☐ If you do not wish to receive any mail from us or other organisations, please tick this box.

☐ If you wish to receive news of other RHP books, but do not want your name on any mailing list provided to other organisations, please tick this box.

Name _____ BOOK

Address _____

_____

_____

Postcode _____ **Phone Number** _____

| Send orders to: **Russell House Publishing Ltd, 4 St. George's House, The Business Park, Uplyme Road, Lyme Regis, Dorset DT7 3LS** Phone: 01297 443 948 Fax: 01297 442 722 |

Regd No. 2881219. All prices are subject to change without prior notice.

Chapter 1
What is child sexual abuse?

A mother remembers

It was 7 o'clock in the morning and as usual about that time my two eldest children used to wake and come into my bed with me until it was time to get up. On this occasion they got into bed one either side of me while I tried to snatch a few more minutes sleep. My oldest children are girl twins and they had just turned four years.

Straight out of the blue one of them said to me "Daddy puts his willy in my bum bum." I was so shocked. I was immediately awake. My brain slotted into working to its full capacity in the same way it engaged when I was in the second stage of labour. I thought, I'm going to have to be very careful here, I must phrase my questions carefully so I don't lead her. I asked her about his penis because I wanted to know whether or not it was erect. I made no real headway so I asked what part of her bottom he put his willy in. She immediately answered in a matter of fact way, "Back part." I finished the conversation by asking whether what she had told me was real or pretend. My other daughter said, "Pretend."

I desperately wanted an explanation for what she had told me. I desperately wanted it to be pretend. But how could it be? Children who are just four don't talk about men putting willies in bums unless they have some knowledge of it. I later came to find out that this cover of 'pretend' was the name of the 'game' covering anything sexually abusive.

I went to the kitchen to make a pot of tea and the children's drinks; while I was there the child who had disclosed put her hand up inside my dressing gown and touched me. All of me wanted someone to say "This isn't true, there is a perfectly logical explanation for this." While emotionally I held onto that hope, logically I knew I had to face up to the truth because everything was falling into place, just like the cogs of machinery lining up so the wheels can start turning. Suddenly there was an explanation for all the disturbed behaviour of the last six months, of the sexualised behaviour of the last few days when she had started kissing me with an open mouth. I thought about the times I had considered sexual abuse and had always dismissed it. I thought about the times I had wondered if it was best for the children that their father and I had split up and maybe if we hadn't, they wouldn't be this unhappy or disturbed. And now the first seeds of reality were telling me that it wasn't that they weren't seeing enough of him, it was that they were seeing him at all.

The two hours wait from the disclosure to when I thought my health visitor would start work was the longest two hours of my life. It was the normal busy, frantic session of getting everybody up, getting everyone dressed, everyone breakfasted etc.. While my body carried on servicing all the children, my mind was in limbo waiting for a professional to tell me what? Either that it wasn't true or where to go from here.

→

Fortunately, my health visitor was on duty, I spoke to her soon after 9.00 a.m.. She said she'd be in a meeting until 11.00 a.m. and then she'd come round. I hadn't mentioned on the phone what it was about, just that it was urgent. I felt so relieved because someone I trusted was about to share this with me.

When she arrived, my son who was only 18 months old, was having his morning sleep. I bribed my daughter, who had disclosed, to look for a chocolate bar in my coat and share it with her sister. Later, when I was telling the health visitor about the disclosure, I realised that she was listening at the door. She knew she had dropped a bombshell and was watching me like a hawk. She must have been very frightened because days later she disclosed that they had been threatened with being thrown onto a lighted bonfire or shot dead by men with guns if they told me about the abuse.

I described the disclosure to the health visitor, her immediate reply was, "Oh no." She went on to explain that children don't lie about being sexually abused because it is outside of their experience. She said she would have to report it and then take it from there. I thought good, we must go forward, this knowledge can't just stop here with the two of us.

The following days and weeks were dreadful. No one seemed to have a clue what I was going through. The child who had disclosed wouldn't let me out of her sight, most of her disclosures were physical, so she was using me as a means to show what had been happening to her. My friends were wonderfully sympathetic and supportive but didn't know any more than I did about how to handle the situation. The children's disturbed behaviour got worse so we all got less sleep. My body reacted as it always does in times of stress by causing me to have the runs. All through the day and night my body was being weakened by the manifestation of physical symptoms caused by the stress. After two weeks and two disclosure interviews I saw a solicitor who was wonderful. Every time she saw me she'd say "Are you all right?" The children's nursery teacher also realised how bad the situation was and said "I should think you are at your wit's end." But apart from them no other professional seemed to realise I was desperate for help. After about 6 weeks a psychiatrist was appointed; her initial help was truly reassuring but it ceased to be once she stepped back from the situation, saying that her role was to observe us as a family and write a report for High Court on her findings.

By sheer luck I was put in contact with Anne. The luck was because two of my friends had just delivered Anne's second baby. When they told Anne about my situation, Anne said she would be happy to help. Once I started meeting with Anne I was immediately getting the quantity and quality of informed support I needed.

Many years on we are now writing this book together. We feel the combined input of a mother who is a professional and a mother whose children have suffered sexual abuse will create a more informative picture. We believe to empower the mother is to empower the child. We are both aware that mothers who discover their children have been sexually abused need immediate access to relevant and helpful information. The aim of this book is to be helpful; it is, of course, impossible for us to include every eventuality, happening or procedure, however, we hope this book goes some way to fulfilling those needs.

Marion

Sexual behaviour with children is against the law. It is a crime. Sexual abuse like all abuse is the abuse of power. Any behaviour which involves a child for the perpetrator's sexual gratification is abusive to that child.

We hope it is helpful to look at what is known about the abuse, the abusers and the children who are victims of the abuse.

1. Child sexual abuse

Child sexual abuse can take a whole variety of forms. There are many different types of abusive behaviours:

- Children being made to watch adults naked or having sex.

- Being shown pornography, either videos or magazines.

- Being groped by someone either over or under their clothes.

- Masturbation of the child or making the child masturbate the adult or themselves or other children.

- Oral-genital contact.

- Penetration of the child's vagina or anus by either a hand, penis or object.

- The use of animals in sexual practices with children.

- Bondage – sexual assaults involving equipment, such as chains.

- Groups of abusers abusing groups of children.

- Abusers getting children to abuse other children.

- Abuse involving rituals designed to frighten children into being victims and then keeping silent.

Children who are abused are in a powerless position because the abuser is usually known to the child and in a position of trust; it often means that the abuse is on-going. It is rarely a one-off event. Therefore the abuse usually continues until either the child is able to tell and is believed, or until someone notices something is wrong and investigates the situation, or the abuser is removed from the child(ren) either leaving voluntarily or being forced to leave. Many children are assaulted several times a week for years.

Child sexual abuse rarely if ever leaves any physical evidence. The only evidence that abuse has happened would be the presence of semen or pubic hair or a witness to the assault. Most of the abusive behaviours we have listed would not leave such evidence. In the absence of evidence that will convince a court, often all the evidence there is, is the word of a child. Then the court has to decide between the word of a child and the word of an adult.

Only a small proportion of cases, once investigated, go on to be referred to the Crown Prosecution Service for a decision about possible court proceedings.

Only a minority of cases are proved in court by the prosecution of a named abuser.

2. Abusers

Most of the abusers who sexually assault children are known to the children beforehand. They get familiar with the children and then abuse that familiarity and trust.

The majority of abusers are men. Some women do abuse but the numbers of female abusers are small. Although the number of female abusers is very small in comparison to the numbers of men who abuse children, the effect on a child is just as painful. The fact that it is less common can leave a child and the mother feeling great isolation.

Abusers come from every class group. There is no one group of people that hasn't had a child abuser in its midst; judges, doctors, teachers, as well as labourers. There is also child sexual abuse in different racial groups. It also happens in both urban and rural settings.

Some abusers deliberately get jobs where they can work officially or as volunteers with children, and then take opportunities to abuse children.

3. The children who are victims of child sexual abuse

Child sexual abuse sadly happens to lots of children. A recent survey in Britain revealed 1 in 20 adults were sexually abused as children by adults known to them. This means in a small school of 200 children with 7 – 8 classes, there may be as many as 10 children who have been sexually abused.

Most abuse begins with very small children. The average age at which abuse starts is said to be 9–10 years. The average age of the children in Cleveland who were said to have been sexually abused was 6 years and the youngest was a 7 months old baby, so children of any age are at risk.

Both boys and girls get abused. The survey estimates that for every three girls who are abused there are two boys abused.

We have learned recently about the very special vulnerability of disabled children. The less power a child has, the more power the abuser has. Some abusers target disabled children as victims, such as very small children, children who can't speak, mentally or physically disabled children. They do this so the children can't tell what is happening to them.

Sexual abuse can leave children vulnerable and injured. Children who haven't received the appropriate and necessary care can remain vulnerable to further abuse. Some abusers look for vulnerable children and seek them out to abuse them. So sadly some abused children are abused by more than one person at more than one time in their lives.

Children who have been abused feel:

- **Isolated:** If something is happening to a child which they feel they can't tell their mum, nor brothers and sisters, nor their favourite teacher, then the child is completely socially and emotionally isolated. This, of course, is what abusers want.

- **Powerless:** Owning your own body is a basic right for everyone, children and adults alike. Abusers do not recognise this right. For children who are abused, the abuse means that they have no say over who touches their body. Denied such a basic right, abused children become convinced they are powerless.

- **Guilty:** Children who are abused are isolated. They not unnaturally conclude that they are the only person in the world this has happened to and so it must be something to do with them, why it happened. They often think it must be their fault. As time passes they feel increasingly guilty, guilty they didn't stop it (as if they could) and guilty they didn't tell (which they couldn't). Often when they do tell, they feel guilty for the disruption and upset that ensues. They imagine this is a consequence of telling, when in fact it is a consequence of the abuser's actions. So at every stage children feel guilty.

What makes people sexually abuse children?

We have deliberately asked this question because we know all mothers whose children have been abused will ask it. Unfortunately answering it isn't as easy. It might help to ask yourself the following questions:

- What is a paedophile seeking?

- What can he get from a child, which he cannot get from an adult?

- What can an adult do, that a child can't?

The answers probably help to point out the powerlessness of children; who are physically smaller, inexperienced, dependent and vulnerable.

Sexual abuse is an abuse of power. If it was just to do with sex the offender would masturbate for sexual gratification or have sex with an adult. Sexual offenders are often in relationships with their wives, partners or other adults whilst they abuse children. It isn't solely to do with sex, it's to do with power.

A probation officer who works with Schedule One offenders was asked this question by mothers in a mother's group. Her answer was she didn't know and furthermore the sexual abusers she worked with didn't know.

Chapter 2
Why didn't my child tell me she/he was being sexually abused?

Your child may disclose to you or disclose to someone else who informs you. Either way the news is devastating and brutal; except for hearing about the death of a child, it is hard to imagine hearing anything worse.

Any mother desperately wants to believe it isn't true. For many mothers the shocking news, the disbelief is accompanied by so many things falling into place and although she still hopes it isn't true, something inside her fears it is. After the initial shock comes the added burden of why your child didn't tell you straight away or why they told someone else and not you.

There are three main reasons why children can't tell about sexual abuse:

- Many children do not have the language and/or the permission to tell about what is happening to them.

- Many children are subject to actual or implied threats not to tell.

- Many children may be unable to recognise the abusive experience as abuse, having been tricked and/or bribed into acquiescence.

These reasons have many facets.

Children do not have the language and/or the permission to tell about what is happening to them

1. Children are too young to use language.
Children who are under the age of 2-3 years do not have the words to describe what is happening. They may only be able to signal their distress and hurt non-verbally, for example, by going rigid at the start of a nappy changing routine (perhaps because that has been a time at which they have been abused). Often problems of interpreting changes in the behaviour of babies and small children who have been abused, is rooted in the fact that we as adults find it so hard to believe that very small children can be sexually assaulted. So adults are reluctant to include sexual abuse as one of their reasons for explaining the changes. Yet we know that sadly, babies and very small children, even as young as under 1 year, do get assaulted.

2. Children with disabilities are an especially vulnerable group.
Children with disabilities are not all the same, they are a heterogeneous or very mixed group and so will have many different reasons of their own why they can't tell. It would be impossible to do justice to all their reasons here, but a few examples illustrate the range and complexities of the reasons why disabled children can't tell.

- A child's disability may be such that she/he does not use language at all.

- Some systems of alternative communication have not included the signs a child would need to tell about sexual abuse.

- Some disabled children are highly dependent on adult care and find it difficult to recognise abuse when all or most of their intimate care is by others.

- When children are dependent, they have no basis for imagining or believing they could successfully object to what happens to them.

- Society can be very rejecting or at best uninterested in disabled children. The children need attention and affection too, and may be especially compliant when attention and affection is offered by an abuser.

3. Children use language but don't have the vocabulary to tell.
Many young children, although they have begun to use language, do not have the words to describe what they see and feel. A child who is 3-4 years old is unlikely to have the words for parts of the body and sexual activities. Such a child will tell with the words she/he has, for example "daddy ... wee wee ... hurts". Small children may well use words which are not recognisable to adults as key words in a description of sexual abuse; one small girl talked about "daddy's strawberry" ... another of "billy". Small children often talk in a quiet, unclear way. Much of what children say when they are first learning to talk is misunderstood or not heard by adults, especially by adults who are not the main care givers and so are not familiar with the child's individual use of language.

4. Children often do not have adult permission to tell about sexual abuse.
We feel we are the first generation of parents to actually come to terms with the magnitude of the problem. Sexual abuse of children has always happened in every class, race and society but it is only recently due to women's gains in power that we are beginning to see how vast the problem is and how we can go about improving things. Our behaviour towards our children has to take into account the legacy that had been left us by our forebears and their attitudes towards parenting, for example, "Children should be seen and not heard" (powerless objects to give pleasure without disruption), and children should obey the person who is caring for them. We therefore educate our children to be fearful of strangers, not fearful of an abusing parent or people appointed by us.

Most parents/teachers agree with the need to warn children about approaches made by strangers. Children are given permission from a very young age to say "no" to strangers, to run away, and to tell about approaches from strangers. Such warnings by implication, though unsaid, do not encourage children to say "no" to familiar adults and to tell about approaches by familiar adults. Yet studies indicate that most perpetrators of child sexual abuse are familiar adults. So, without specific teaching children are unlikely to feel able to reject and to tell about an approach by a known adult.

5. Children are taught to obey parents/adults.
In our society, children are continually made aware, at home, at school, and in the community, of their powerlessness vis-a-vis adults. Children are taught to obey their parents/adults in ways which can leave them vulnerable. For example, most of us can recall being propelled to kiss good night to grandad or a relative, and on displaying some reluctance being told "Don't be silly ... don't hurt his/her feelings ... you won't get any pocket money/sweets if you don't ...". The message is that you should do as you are told by adults and that you are not entitled to say who touches your body. Children need prevention work done with them which helps them to understand that they have a right to say who touches their body.

6. Children who cannot trust a parent/familiar adult do not know to whom they can go.

Most adults who sexually abuse children are known to the children beforehand. For the child to whom this is happening, there will seem to be no one to tell. If a child can't trust adults she/he knows, then she/he is unlikely to trust any adults. Again, without specific teaching children will not know to whom to go for help.

7. Children who are abused by peers or staff in residential settings.

Children can live away from home for a variety of reasons. They may have physical, learning disabilities or emotional difficulties, which lead to a residential placement, or family difficulties which can be such that they have to live in a children's home or in alternative family placements, being fostered or adopted. Children not living in their family of origin can have a whole range of reasons why they can't tell. A few examples illustrate the problem:

- A child can fear that, having been placed away from home, telling about sexual abuse will jeopardise a placement which has accepted them.

- A child who has been placed because of difficulties following sexual abuse may believe, if it should happen again in the residential placement, that he/she is to blame for it happening twice or will not be believed if she/he tells a second time.

- If the abuser is a member of a staff team that runs the establishment, a child can fear staff loyalties will result in no one believing.

- If the placement had taken time to arrange, the child may fear telling about sexual abuse will mean there will be nowhere else to go.

- The ethos of the placement can be such in terms of staff and children's behaviours, that a child sexually assaulted in that setting can be confused about whether this is intrinsic to the placement, a part of what happens to everyone in that place, and so not something that can be complained about.

8. Children may well have told or think they have told.

When children recognise the uncomfortable feelings abuse gives them or realise that what is happening to them is not right, they may well try to tell. Often children try to tell in tentative or oblique ways – for example, the child who asks to stay behind after school rather than go straight home, or the child who talks of not liking being tickled, or the child who talks of being visited by a monster in the night. Children may often feel that they have told and that what they have said has been disbelieved or ignored. If children believe what they say is discounted or not heard, they are less likely to try to tell in future.

9. Some children say they don't remember.

This is a frequently given reason by children and adults with histories of abuse, for not telling at the time about being sexually assaulted. One way some children survive the experience of sexual abuse is to not think about it, "to not remember", when they are away from the situations/people who abuse them. This becomes a way of survival; keeping going, preserving some sense of normality or sanity, and avoiding jeopardising the situations/people that are non-abusing and that they value. For example, a child can reason that school is the only place where I am safe and don't get abused, and where I can feel the same as others; if I tell, everything will change and then what will I have?

Children are subject to actual or implied threats not to tell

10. Children may witness violence in the home.

If a child witnesses violence committed in the home against her/his mother and/or siblings, such a child will not need to be hurt directly or even threatened, to be compliant. The understanding that they too could be hurt is clear.

11. Children may be subject to threats of violence.

As a child grows older and begins to realise the abusive nature of what is happening and begins to try to say no, they may be subject to threats. Often children will use the concern or reactions of others to try to protect themselves; for example, "My teacher keeps asking me what's wrong" ... or ... "We'll be in trouble if we get caught". Children can be told: "I'll kill you if you tell". Children are completely unaware how they may be protected from such a threat. Sadly, some children cannot be protected, Keighley Barton was murdered by her stepfather when she tried to tell.

12. Children may well not tell the other parent/care giver/or significant adult because of specific threats.

Children who are abused are often made aware, by their abuser, of the precarious balance maintained by the child's silence. A child can't tell if she/he is told, "Don't tell, you'll upset your mum/it will make your mum ill/your teacher will know what kind of person you are ... etc.". So specific threats can be made against people, pets, or things that they love, which ensure their silence.

13. The threats which silence a child can be implicit.

The abuser need not appear violent to the child nor utter explicit threats, for a child to still feel threatened. A child can perceive implicit threats from a variety of sources:

- From the fact that the abuser isolates the child from caring, non-abusing adults and peers.

- The abuser may change during the abuse from the way he appears to others and in other settings.

- The abuser may hurt the child.

- The child may have drawn his/her own conclusions about the link between the abuse and venereal disease or Aids or pregnancy or promiscuity, of which 'society' disapproves.

14. Children silenced by racism.

Children who are from minority ethnic groups are only too frequently aware of the racism there is in our society at personal and institutional levels. If children feel rejected or not valued on account of their colour, culture, religion, language, dress, then that process of rejection also silences them from speaking out about sexual abuse. Children can be silenced by racism in many ways; a few examples underline how the process works:

- If a child feels rejected or undervalued on account of his/her racial group then she/he may conclude that it is unlikely anyone outside his/her group will believe or care about the abuse.

- A child who feels rejected or undervalued on account of his/her racial group may have seen a parent racially harassed for no cause and fear if she/he tells then she/he will be blamed and harassed too.

- A black child who is abused by a white adult/child may fear that if she/he were to tell, that the white adult/child would deny what he has done and that his word would be believed before that of a black child.

- A black child who is abused by a black adult/child may fear that to tell of the abuse would not only expose what has happened, but also provide people who are racist with additional triggers to punish the child and/or black people.

- Few local authorities demonstrate as much zeal towards equal opportunities policies of staff recruitment as they do towards child protection. So a child from a minority ethnic group may be aware that the social worker, doctor, police officer, psychologist, that they meet after telling about abuse will all be white. The message then is that child protection is what white people do. Black children could be empowered by having it demonstrated to them, that child protection is a concern for all non-abusing adults of all races.

15. The abuser's strategies to bribe the children may also serve to silence them.
Abusers quite deliberately use a variety of strategies to trick or bribe children into acquiescence during abuse. They are often extremely skilled in the strategies they use, drawing the child to them in a way which appeals to each child. Some abusers deliberately use tricks and bribes of which non-abusing, caring adults in the child's life would disapprove. When the child has been tricked and bribed, the child then feels she/he can't tell because they have done something which they know their parents don't like. For example, a group of boys aged 8–13 years were tricked into going to the flat of the local postman, who was also a paedophile, with bribes of alcoholic drink, cigarettes, sweets, and money. They told their parents lies about where they were going and/or truanted from school to go to his flat and get these bribes. When he later began to sexually assault them, they felt they couldn't tell because they had already done so many things that they knew their parents would not allow, that they would be in trouble and blamed for the situation and for being abused; as one boy said, "It's my fault, I should never have gone to his house in the first place", so the very bribes an abuser uses also become threats to silence children.

16. Children believe that her/his acquiescence and silence protects siblings from abuse.
Children are isolated by their abuse from their non-abusing parent and their siblings. The thought that while their abuser continues to assault her/him, sisters and/or brothers will not be assaulted, can be enough to keep a child from telling. A child can often be completely unaware that sisters/brothers are being abused too. The knowledge that this is happening or that an abuser is turning to a younger child can show a child that silence has not protected siblings, and perhaps prompt her/him to tell.

17. Children deduce that sexual abuse is socially reprehensible.
Even a young child can deduce that what is happening to her/him is not to be talked about. Young children can learn quickly that some things daddy does when no one else is there, are never talked about to mummy when she comes home, whereas other things daddy tells mummy. Children take their cues from adults. As children get older, reports in newspapers, publicity for ChildLine, talk with peers,

will leave them with no doubt that what is happening to them is wrong. Children who have kept the secret for a long time feel implicated by their silence and fear the reactions of others, and so can't tell.

18. The alternatives to being abused are unknown.

Often an abuser will tell a child that if she/he tells, he (the abuser) will have to go to prison; the family will be split up, the children will have to go into care; social workers and the police will come. The implications are always that such consequences are worse than being abused. Children have no basis on which to evaluate their situation. For example, they have no reason to assume that other adults will not abuse them too. Children thus fear they will only exchange one kind of unhappiness for another.

19. The alternatives to being abused are known.

Ironically, it may be that a child who is being abused is aware of the consequences of telling about the abuse and is silenced by this. Children can learn about the consequences of telling about the abuse in a variety of ways: a child can know another child who was abused, read newspapers or hear television accounts of a child who was abused and who told; and see what then happened to the child as no encouragement for him/her to tell. Child abuse casework is full of examples of children who have told about abuse only to be disbelieved; received into care; separated from siblings; abused by a different person at a different time. Where prosecutions have failed, etc., a child may be silenced by feeling she/he knows what the alternatives to being abused are and these are no inducement to tell.

Children may be unable to recognise the abusive experience as abuse, having been tricked or bribed into acquiescence

20. The child may only have ever known abuse.

It may be that a child has only ever known abuse. If this is the case then the child would have no experiences on which to expect love, kindness, and protection. For a young child whose view of the world is egocentric and very present orientated, there would be nothing with which to compare what was happening with what happens to other people. It is only when children are older, they begin to visit the houses of friends without their parents, are able to read about different home situations, and begin to share their lot with their peers. It is then that children begin to understand that what is happening to them, does not happen to everyone. The young child who has only ever known abuse may be unable to recognise what is happening as abuse and that she/he can tell about it.

21. When several children are abused and aware of each other's abuse, confusion about abuse happens.

There are situations where several children are abused and they are aware of the abuse of the other children; such situations can include abuse by a paedophile, by a sex ring, when children are away from home. The children can become confused. They can wonder "If it is happening to all of us then it can't be so bad". Additionally, they can be confused by each child's inability to tell into wondering whether it isn't okay if no one seems to object. Paradoxically, they can feel completely frozen into silence and inaction when no-one else seems to object or be able to stop it from happening.

22. Abusers may convince the children that the abuse is part of an affectionate parenting role.

Children, by virtue of their innocence, can be tricked into not telling and keeping secrets. They can be told "This is daddy's special game", "This is the way daddy loves you". They would have no experience to know otherwise. This is particularly the case with younger children whose experiences are concrete and more orientated in the present. Their experiences are based on egocentric perceptions, bound up as they are with identification with parent/adult models, and so their experiences do not permit them to know otherwise.

23. The abusive experience may be all the children receive in response to their need to be held and cuddled.

All children (and adults) need to feel wanted, valued, cared for and held. A child who is being abused may well see such abuse as an inevitable price for being held and cuddled, and may not want to tell for fear of losing the comfort they do have. For if a child were to tell what is happening, who then would hold and cuddle him/her?

24. Children may well love their abuser and be reluctant to betray him/her.

Any adult who can enjoin a young child to silence while systematically abusing that child is a skillful adult. The idea that such adults will always be viewed by the children they abuse as threatening is naive. Many are able to establish a relationship with a child such that the child will love them and be reluctant to betray them. This gives some indication of the far-reaching consequences of abuse, that children can and do develop the strength to protect adults. When abuse occurs the implicit duties of parents/adults to care for and protect children are put aside and the impulses of the adult cut across the children's needs.

25. Children may well have the position of 'favoured' child emotionally and/or materially.

Most insidious of all is the fact that abuse may well take place in a context in which a child's bodily sensations are aroused and/or the child is rewarded for her/his acquiescence. Sexual responsiveness is essentially learned behaviour. Children can become completely overwhelmed and confused by their own responses to the extent that they internalise those responses and see them as indicative of their responsibility for the abuse. They may see their own sexual behaviour as a cause of the abuse. Some children may need support to recognise the abuse of sensual touch, and be freed from feelings of self doubt and guilt on account of their own responses. They need to see their responses as the consequences of abuse, not the cause.

The reasons that children have for not being able to tell are different for every child and change over time according to:

- age/developmental stage
- gender
- cultural/ethnicity issues
- abilities/disabilities

- temperament

- the identity of the abuser

- the nature of the abuse

- the duration of the abuse

- what they imagine will be the reactions to their telling.

What does become clear when you think about the reasons why children can't tell is that they have lots of good reasons why they can't tell and so few, if any, reasons for telling. Here is a list of reasons for not being able to tell, made by a group of girls aged 10–14 years.

Reasons why children can't tell about sexual abuse

1. Because their dad or the abuser would box them up.

2. People might think they are lying.

3. People might think they are dirty.

4. Brothers/sisters might think the child wants more attention.

5. Guilty.

6. Don't tell because their mum and dad are getting married and don't want them to break up.

7. She or he might be threatened by the abuser

8. He or she might be too little to understand.

9. The child doesn't want to hurt people's feelings.

10. The child doesn't want the abuser to go to prison.

11. If the children tell it will spoil the relations with his/her mum.

12. Some children can't tell because they think the silence protects the brother or sister …

13. Or because adults don't listen.

14. Some children don't know what words to use.

15. A child may feel that they have to be loyal to their parents.

16. Can't tell until mum's in a good mood and some mums never get in a good mood, or dads.

17. Can't get mum on her own to tell her.

18. Some children have a handicap so they can't tell (deaf, etc.).

19. Children have been asked to keep it a secret.

20. Some children tricked into believing it's their fault.

21. Some boys or girls have been given money not to tell or are blackmailed.

22. Abuse makes some children feel sexual so they feel guilty.

23. Some children know what will happen if they tell.

24. They might feel they are the only one.

→

---

25. Some children are tricked into feeling they enjoyed it.

26. The abuser may well have threatened someone else in the family.

27. Because the abuser will deny it ever happened.

28. The abuser could be someone official (like a social worker, teacher or policeman) and the child thinks no one will ever believe him/her.

29. Some abusers pay the children to keep quiet.

30. Some children don't tell teachers because they will talk about it in the staff room.

31. Some children can't tell because their mums don't care.

32. Some children can't tell because they want to forget.

If your child has been able to tell you or someone that he/she has been sexually assaulted, the child has faced huge pressures not to tell and probably broken months or years of silence to do so. It is important to understand how hard it has been for your child to tell and to be glad she/he could do so. If it was not you that your child told, you need to respect the choice your child made. Children have their own reasons which are good ones at the time and make sense from their point of view. By demonstrating to your child that you understand and respect their choice you will hopefully open up a discussion in which your child will learn that not only have they got your permission to talk about the abuse, but you want to hear about it and will respond in a caring and protective way. This should help your child to talk to you more in the future. One mother of an abused child wrote the following about the disclosure she made of her own abuse as a child.

After disclosure

The question was what would I have liked to have happened after I told someone about the abuse? Well, I don't know. I have not thought about it, my only wish was for it to stop.

The only thing that I ever wanted out of life was to be loved by someone, anyone. To be held and told they would make it all right, to be made to feel that I was a person and I mattered, that I was loveable. I wanted just to be treated as others were.

Toys and objects did not matter to me, I did not dream of rich or famous parents just normal loving ones.

I suppose my dreams of childhood are the same dreams as my adulthood now.

Judy

Why was it my child?

The simplest answer to this is; it was because your child happened to be there. Another child could be in a class with an excellent teacher or in a youth group with an innovative worker and those children are advantaged for no other reason than they happened to be there. In the same way your child has been exposed to the worst adults do to children. The child is never to blame in any way and has no responsibility for what has happened. Take this book with you, read it and walk on.

Chapter 3
Why didn't I know?

Perhaps the hardest thought in the days, months, years, after the abuse of your child becomes known, is why didn't I know? This section aims to explore some ideas which we hope will help you think about this question, and realise that it was virtually impossible for you to know at the time that your child was being assaulted. In thinking about this question, we would like to develop three ideas.

The sexual abuse of a child is always the responsibility of the person who committed the assault

The first idea is to look at why the sexual abuse of a child is always the responsibility of the person who committed that assault. There are four reasons why it was the abuser's fault.

1. Sexual assaults against children are against the law. They are crimes for which those who commit them are responsible and if found guilty they have to face the consequences of their wrong doing. So the law actually states that sexual assaults against children are wrong and that the abuser is to blame.

2. Sexual assaults against children are usually committed by adults or older children. Adults have to be responsible for what they do. Unless it is recognised that the adult is incapable of being responsible and controlling himself, in which case that person needs treatment and supervision. Our society sees adults, and children approaching adulthood, as having to be responsible for what they do.

3. It is clear that abusers are not driven by uncontrollable urges which might be thought to make them less responsible for what they do. They show in their daily lives that they can and do control themselves in a whole variety of ways. They rarely openly break other laws or abuse children when they are being observed. So they can control themselves and they are responsible when they don't.

4. It is also clear that the vast majority of abusers know what they have done is morally wrong. They go to great lengths to conceal what they do. Quite frequently a review of the abuse of a child over time will reveal the extent of the planning by the abuser to get opportunities to abuse without detection. Some abusers choose their partners or plan to get jobs, to get access to children who they can then abuse. Also, they go to great lengths to ensure that the child doesn't tell, which was discussed earlier. So their behaviour actually evidences great self control and a clear understanding that they know they are doing wrong.

It never ever is the fault of the child to whom this has happened

The second idea is to look at why it never ever is the fault of the child that this has happened to them. Four reasons emerge:

5. The adults and young people who sexually assault children are older than the children they abuse. As a society we teach children to look to older people for what is right and wrong, and for guidance on how to behave. So children trust adults to know what is right and wrong, and so if an adult tells them to do something they will comply, often even when they think it is wrong or they don't want to do it. Children are taught to defer to older people by us all.

6. People who sexually assault children are usually bigger and stronger than the children they abuse. When children are asked/told/threatened to do something by someone bigger and stronger, they really have no choices. They have to do as they are told and cannot be blamed for doing so, even if they knew it was wrong. We need to recognise how many abused children have done as they were told by the abuser as a means of self-preservation which was sensible for them at that time.

7. In our society, adults have recognised positions of power over children. There are so many signs of our power visible to children. We tell children when to get up and go to bed, we decide what children eat, when they can go out, when they can have keys and money. We are able to tell better lies and to be believed more than the children are, so abused children can never be to blame for deferring to a power differential which is present and effective in every other aspect of their lives.

8. Adults know about sex. We know about the law as it relates to sex, we know about a range of sexual practices, and we know about the feelings sex brings. Children do not know any of this. If the abuse goes on over a long period of time, a child may come to know more of this and feel that they did know about sex and so might be partly to blame. Abusers take advantage of the difference between them as adults and their child victims in terms of their knowledge and understanding of sex. The child cannot be blamed for what she/he does not know and understand.

Mothers rarely know at the time it is happening that their child is being sexually assaulted by someone they know and trust

The third idea is to look at why mothers rarely know at the time it is happening that their child is being sexually assaulted by someone they know and trust. Four reasons underpin this for most mothers.

9. Children can't tell about sexual abuse. They are often too young and/or don't have the language to tell what is happening to them. They may have been

threatened, either explicitly or implicitly, not to tell in ways that have ensured their silence. They may well also have been tricked and bribed into not being able to recognise that they have been/are being abused and so see no reason to tell their mother.

10.   Our society has been very slow to recognise that sexual assaults on children happen as frequently as they do, and that children are most in danger from people that they know who are then able to abuse their positions of familiarity and trust. Even when abuse is recognised, society puts up all kinds of defences as a way of avoiding the reality of child sexual abuse: such as the paediatrician was over zealous, the social worker got it wrong, the child is lying, the adult survivor has false memory syndrome, it's all the fault of video nasties. If our society has such defences, it is no surprise mothers don't believe it could happen. Mothers are part of society, hardly a minority group; most women become mothers. There is no reason why we should have some miraculous knowledge from which the rest of society hasn't benefited. Why should mothers believe it any more than anyone else?

11.   Despite what we do now know about child sexual assaults, one defence of society is such that there is no real public support for a campaign to teach people and warn children about the problem. Most schools and nurseries run 'Don't go with a stranger' campaigns, but find the idea of prevention work for children about sexual assaults by adults they know much more controversial, and often too difficult to tackle at all. So if there is no support to teach children and families about the problems and the warning signs that there may be, then what are mothers to look for? Often mothers will say, once the abuse of their child is known, that there were signs something was wrong and that with hindsight it all makes sense and they feel they should have known. Those thoughts are not the same as knowing at the time and shouldn't be confused as such by the mother, or the professionals. Mothers largely have no basis on which they could have known.

12.   Abusers are clever. The fact that they are able to enjoin children to silence over years and avoid being observed as they sexually assault those children, attests to their capacity to plan and organise people and events. This level of deliberate and calculated abuse of dependent children is actually unthinkable. It is particularly unthinkable and beyond belief for mothers as it is usually perpetrated by people whom they know and trust. People who abuse children are often people on whom the mother depends for her own needs; such as a partner, baby-sitter, friend, relative, professional. So the idea that a person you know and trust is systematically planning and then sexually assaulting your child is literally unthinkable and beyond belief.

Nearly all abuse goes on for a period of time. The very fact that all mothers ask this question proves it isn't just you or only an odd individual who wasn't being responsive or observant by not realising what was going on. One only has to go to a mother's group to hear all the mothers present ask the same question. We hope the following list will reinforce an understanding of why it was virtually impossible to know at the time.

Reasons why it is virtually impossible for mothers to know at the time that their child is being sexually assaulted

- Most of the publicity suggests strangers or weirdos assault children not people the mothers know.

- The abuser is usually someone known to the mother and so in a position of trust and responsibility: so he would be the last person the mother would suspect, e.g. a partner, a friend etc..

- The abuser often manoeuvres to prevent any closeness between the mother and her children.

- The abuser goes to great lengths to demonstrate his apparent concern and care for the children – buying presents, taking them out – and this can deceive a mother.

- Mothers and the general public are not given detailed information which would make them more vigilant and aware of the reality and possibility that their children could be assaulted by a person in their trust.

- Children can't tell their mothers because the abusers threaten/bribe the children to say nothing.

- The warning signs that children use to show that they are being assaulted are often non-specific; for example, complaints of stomach ache, nightmares, having a rash, a child walking differently, headaches, a child pulling her hair out.

- The abuser rationalises signs the children show to the mother to the point where she loses faith in her own judgement.

- The mother may be a lone parent and is preoccupied with caring for the children and working and perhaps planning to marry someone, so she is unable to notice changes in her child's behaviour or feels they are explained by current family stresses/changes.

- The abuser, if a partner, heaps blame on the mother for not satisfying him or for being sick, to such an extent that she has no sense of self-esteem and believes whatever seems to be going wrong for her children is her fault.

- Child sexual assault is hard for a mother to detect because the abuser is so clever and plans it so well.

- No-one, including mothers, could imagine the ways and circumstances that abusers assault children; for example, in the same bed while the mother is asleep, when there is a house full of people, in the toilet, the kitchen or the bathroom.

- If the mother suspects and the husband/partner is violent she can fear to speak out.

→

- A mother may have some suspicions that her child is being assaulted but when she approaches an agency they won't act without evidence or full disclosure, so what can she do?

- Some abusers realise agencies have concerns and so prevent professionals having access to the mother; for example by taking mail before she gets it, being there at appointments and so silencing the professional who fears tipping the abuser off about their concerns.

- Even when children do make full disclosures, mothers see reports of court cases where men have been named as abusers and yet make successful applications for access and custody.

- Mothers are not listened to in this society; they are not seen as having status and doing a worthwhile job.

- Professionals don't trust mothers enough to arrange to speak to a mother on her own and share their concerns with her.

- The state stacks the odds against mothers believing their children, because there is no support for women who want to take themselves and their children away from fears of abuse. There needs to be hostels, support for child care, counselling support, legal support to get custody of their children etc..

By: Ruth   Pamela
**   Caroline   Susan**

We believe this question of why didn't I know is inevitable and difficult for mothers. We also believe there are reasons why mothers don't know. We wish you the strength to believe these reasons and not to let this question add to your burdens as you walk with your children away from abuse and to a better life for you all.

Chapter 4
What happens when a child tells?

Once a child tells, the speed a mother has to work at to accept facts, change her conceptions and understand the law is very fast. She has to take in and absorb information at a fantastic rate in order to keep up with her children's needs and not just be washed along with a tide of events over which she has no control. To begin with, things often move slowly while agencies are setting things up and the mother can be left isolated and unsupported, holding on to endless bombshells which explode constantly and with everyone seemingly unaware. This in turn can lead to a divide when discussing things with friends; they can't travel at the speed the mother must. The situation can feel similar to the one when you become a mother for the first time. It's then often easier to discuss matters with other mothers instead of your single friends with whom you have been friends for much longer. It can't be helped, you have a knowledge women who aren't parents don't have. In the same way when you discover your child(ren) has been sexually abused, the pain and grief you go through, subjects you to an experience only another mother in the same situation fully understands. This can lead to you feeling isolated, even if you are surrounded by friends and family. Some can be completely honest and say they find discussing the subject on a personal level too difficult. Others can try to cope while they are practically crippled with embarrassment. Some cope well. If you can share your feelings with another mother or a group of mothers it can be mutually very supportive. Professional help can be invaluable but professionals are not swimming about in it; they are not personally involved and can get up and leave.

After the initial disclosure it is not unusual for the mother to swing between believing her child(ren) and believing the alleged abuser who may be denying everything or minimising what the child has said. This is especially likely if the abuser is the mother's partner or a close relative. Social workers need to take on board how difficult this shift in belief is; how hard it is for a mother to accept that a person she trusted and relied upon has violated her trust and her child(ren). It is at this time the mother is most in need of support to believe what has happened. It isn't only coming to believe the abuse has happened, it can mean a complete change of circumstances. These changes can include: the children who have not been abused not accepting what has happened and putting pressure on her; the complete disruption of the family; and huge changes in financial and housing issues. One mother wrote about the financial and housing upheavals she faced.

The hidden cost

For a long time I felt bitter at the loss of nearly all our possessions. For the first week we had only what we stood up in. I felt bitter at Social Services who seemed oblivious of the pain of having no night-clothes, no change of underwear, no pan even to boil water in for a cup of coffee, no plates or cutlery to eat with. When they arrested him I broke back into the house, conned the car keys out of him and took a car load of clothes, kitchen equipment and toys. We could start living a bit again.

→

I tried hard to get more of our things, not with much success. When we left the hotel to go into a PSL property no-one asked if we had bedding and this time I managed to con some bedding out of him.

Today, two years later, we have little of what I originally salvaged – the clothes have worn out mostly, and I've managed to buy better bedding. We still have most of the kitchen things. But I got a shock recently. I asked my eldest daughter whether another mother's children would get over the trauma of using the furniture from the house where the abuse took place. She talked with bitterness of the plates which would catch her unawares with memories of our old house, of him, of what had happened. She says the worst part is that these familiar objects bring up these memories so unexpectedly when her defences are down. She would really prefer not to have them around. She realises how difficult this would be, which is why she hadn't mentioned it.

From this I would question how much this is a factor in how well and how quickly the victim comes to terms with the memories. Has anyone done any studies? Is there anyone prepared to help with the cost of this. Could we help each other by swapping goods – a sofa which holds memories for one child might not have the same feeling for another.

Caroline

Mothers needs care and understanding, not the threat of judgement at a time of crisis. Belief that child sexual abuse has happened in one's family is for most women a process which takes time, and for which they need support.

The law surrounding child protection is complicated and you will inevitably find yourself becoming more and more aware of the choices you have to make when you are discussing the situation with the professionals involved. Everyone will have an awareness; no one will need educating in order for a conversation to progress. This will not be the case when talking to family and friends. They won't know and you can find yourself having to explain the legal situation time and time again. Whereas it is vital you fully understand the situation because your children's sanity is dependent on you making the right decision, your friends and relatives won't have to take things in with the same intensity. For some extraordinary reason some people think you're seeking their advice, whereas what you usually need is someone to listen and take in the information so you can discuss the situation with them as it is, and not how they imagine it to be.

Mothers who are looking after children who have recently disclosed are under enormous pressure. They have to cope with their own grief, help their children to come to terms with what has happened in a positive way and then feel the added burden of being judged and scrutinised by very powerful organisations.

Some mothers who are helping their children cope with the effects of sexual abuse, were themselves sexually abused. For those who were unable to disclose or those who disclosed and weren't believed, coping the second time around can cut deeper than when it was them. The worse that happened to them as a child has now happened to their own child. Feelings that were buried in order to cope and carry on can come flooding back and be overwhelming. There can also be the difficulty of coping with family members who prefer to live a lie. The mother can be placed in the situation of believing and protecting her children while supporting others who are refusing to believe it happened before, when the mother was a child, and/or refusing to believe it has happened again. Being on the receiving end of advice from the non-believer is a cruel fate.

The trouble would seem to be that the moment the professional agencies become aware of alleged child sexual abuse, the person who goes under the greatest scrutiny is the main care giver, usually the mother. Even if the situation is handled with sensitivity it can be shattering for a mother to cope with the feeling that people could feel she made up the allegation or she herself is under suspicion of being an abuser or about to be judged as a mother.

The very least most mothers feel is that they have to present excellent standards of the traditional caring and cleaning type. A mother can fear she will not be believed or have her children taken away from her. So at the very time she is stretched to her limits to cope with the disclosure and all that goes with it, she then also has to make a super human effort to 'show' herself to be a model parent. Preparing for an official visit in your own home can increase the strain on an already over stressed mother. Your situation will probably be that you have devoted your time to helping your children through their trauma and the fact you are sticking to the kitchen floor is very low on the list of priorities.

> When my health visitor phoned to say she, the social worker and a police officer from the Child Protection Unit would have the initial meeting at my house at 9.15 a.m., I remember saying, "Oh great, the house will look as if a bomb has hit it." She said, "Well that won't matter will it?" It didn't matter to her because she already knew me and her picture was formed. I was under no illusions that the others would draw their first impressions from all the information that surrounded them and a chaotic environment wouldn't help. I spent the whole of the day before the meeting clearing up and cleaning. Presenting a picture of an orderly caring mother in an orderly caring home.
>
> It wasn't until afterwards I realised I could have got away with doing a lot less. I could have chosen which room we were going to sit in and cleared it up, cleaned the loo and the passage between the two rooms, washed four coffee mugs thoroughly and then shut all the other doors in the house!
>
> **Marion**

The reverse would seem to be true for most abusers; most aren't prosecuted, most do nothing to come to terms with the fact they are abusers and harmful to society. Most do nothing to help the children and non-abusing parents through their grief. Most don't have to make any effort in any way to do anything. All that usually happens is they are forbidden to see the children they have abused in an unsupervised capacity.

The Children Act (1989) goes a long way towards improving the rights of children but we have even further to go as a society before the real issues over the balance of power and the abuse of power are addressed.

It may be that some of the things your child has told you seem unbelievable. What should you do? Should you challenge them or accept what they say as true. We believe that the mother's role is not that of judge and jury, her role is that of carer. We therefore suggest that you do not judge what your child has said. It will probably be that you can make your own assessment concerning the validity of the disclosure given the other information you are receiving at the time, like their mood, how difficult it was for them to tell you, what their behaviour was like before and after telling you. Listen to your child and talk about what they have told you if they want you to. Whatever your child says make a note of it and discuss it with your social worker or the child's therapist. For example your child could name another abuser which you find hard to believe; it's important that that information is passed on.

This section looks in some detail at the responses of professional agencies such as, Social Services, the Police, and Health to child sexual abuse. These agencies have to act according to the law as laid down in the Children Act 1989* and the legislation with regard to sexual offences. The stated aim of the Act was to achieve a better balance between the duty of the state to protect children and the need to allow parents to challenge state intervention in the upbringing of their children. The Act also aimed to encourage greater partnership between local authorities and parents, and to encourage a greater use of voluntary arrangements. The legal framework of the Act shapes the responses of all professional workers in Child Protection work.

The Local Authority in which you live has a legal duty to investigate when it is believed that a child has been/is being abused. This duty is in the Act in the following words:

The Children Act 1989

"Section 47

Where a local authority –

A.   Are informed that a child who lives, or is found, in their area

    i)   is the subject of an EPO (an Emergency Protection Order);

    or

    ii)   have reasonable cause to suspect that a child who lives, or is found, in their area is suffering, or is likely to suffer, significant harm,

the Authority shall make, or cause to be made, such enquiries as they consider necessary to enable them to decide whether they should take any action to safeguard or promote the child's welfare."

Obviously much hinges on what is meant by 'reasonable cause' in terms of what prompts a local authority to act. There is no specified detail in the Act about this. While there may be differences between authorities, reasonable cause in terms of sexual abuse may include the following:

---

* This Act applies, on the whole, to England and Wales. Similar duties apply in Scotland under the Children (Scotland) Act 1995.

1. A child says she/he has been touched in a sexual way.

2. A third party says a child has been touched in a sexual way. A third party could be another child, any adult, or an anonymous letter or telephone call.

3. A child with genital injuries/or medical problems consistent with possible sexual abuse.

4. A child who talks or acts in a sexualised way which is different from what one would expect for a child of that age, gender, ability, culture, and temperament.

5. Where a Schedule One Offender is living in the same household or having regular contact with a child. A Schedule One offender is a person who has been convicted under the 1933 Act of serious crimes against children such as murder, bodily harm and sexual assaults.

In addition to the Children Act, each local authority has written Child Protection procedures which all agencies must follow if a professional suspects/knows that child abuse is happening. The procedures give clear definitions of what constitutes child abuse. Here is one such definition:

Sexual abuse

"Sexual abuse is defined as the occurrence of a sexual act/s involving a child which is committed by an adult. (e.g. five years difference). It is recognised, however, that children can abuse other children and the issue is whether informed consent was freely given or whether coercion or exploitation* was used when initiating the act – this latter event is regarded as abusive.

Sexual acts include:

Direct sexual acts – genital or anal contact, child's or adult's, penetration; oral, vaginal or anal, and other acts which involve the child as the object of sexual gratification (e.g., bondage, ejaculation on the child's skin).

Indirect sexual acts – genital exposure, pornographic activity involving children in the production thereof.

* Exploitation refers to the balance of power between the child and other person, at the time that the activity just occurred. This exploitation is considered to have occurred if the activity was unwarranted when first begun and involved a misuse of conventional age, authority or gender differentials."

Given that the local authority has this clear legal duty to investigate when it has reasonable cause to suspect a child is suffering or is likely to suffer significant harm, all local authorities have to have Child Protection procedures. These are written procedures which tell staff what action they should take. All staff in Social Services, the Police and Health departments, who work with children and families should have had some training in the procedures and a copy of them. The extent to which staff follow the procedures is checked by managers in the departments. The overall responsibility for the procedures being followed and reviewed on a regular basis, rests with the Area Child Protection Committee (ACPC). The ACPC is a committee of representatives of all agencies whose workers deal with children and families, such as family doctors, hospital doctors, health visitors, social workers, probation officers, teachers, education social workers, the police, and voluntary groups such as the National Society for the Prevention of Cruelty to Children (NSPCC). Some local authorities and Child Protection agencies produce leaflets/booklets to help children and families understand the process of an investigation and case conferences. It is useful to check if these are available in your area/local authority. All local authorities and Child Protection agencies should have formal complaints procedures. You can ask for a copy of these if you are unhappy with how you or your children are being treated.

Each local authority has its own set of Child Protection procedures. They are all largely similar. What follows is a brief overview of the sequence of the procedures to help you understand what happens when a child tells or someone suspects that a child has been sexually assaulted.

---

1.   Someone thinks a child has been/is being sexually abused
This could be on the basis of any of the five points made earlier.

---

2.   Social Services is told
Referrals go to a duty social worker. This person may be part of a children and families social work team or part of a specialist Child Protection investigation team. This worker is supervised by a manager who has the responsibility to ensure that the Child Protection procedures are followed and who supervises the investigation. The duty social worker will ask the referrer for as much detail as she/he is able to give. Basic details needed are the name, date of birth, address of the child, and the reasons for the concerns. Any additional details such as the family composition and the names of other people involved with the child, are useful.

---

3.   Agency checks are instigated
The duty social worker will then instigate agency checks. This means ringing all agencies who may have had dealings with the child and/or family members to see what is known about the family. These checks will include; the police, probation service, the child's school, education social work service, the family doctor, hospital records, social services' records, housing etc.. The reason for making these checks is to establish whether other professionals/agencies also have concerns. These concerns may not be specific or seem significant until they are included in a wider picture. Much will depend on the information that comes from these checks. There are three outcomes possible at this stage.

4.

4.1 No further action
The decision to take no further action is usually made if the concerns of the referrer are very limited and unfounded, and if there are not any other concerns about the child and/or family from other agencies. This decision will be taken by the worker dealing with the referral and his/her manager. The referrer will be informed of the decision.

4.2 Immediate response
Social Services will act immediately if a child has a non-accidental injury, makes a direct disclosure of sexual abuse, or is left alone. In these instances there will be an investigation. If the concerns indicate that a criminal act has been committed then this investigation will be carried out jointly by social services and the police.

4.3 Planning meeting
The duty officer and manager may decide that there are concerns about the welfare of the child. While there may not be enough concerns to start a Child Protection investigation the worker has the option of calling a Planning Meeting to which workers from agencies who know the child and family will be invited to share their information, discuss concerns, and decide on the best action for the child. A Planning Meeting can decide either:

either   or

No further action
The decision not to investigate will be made if there is not enough evidence at that time to begin an investigation. What may happen is that a worker from a particular agency is given the task of monitoring the child's situation, with the possibility that if there are heightened concerns, then these will be referred.

This planned monitoring of a child will be reviewed within a given timescale. It will be at the Review that a decision is made; as to whether there will be no further action, or that concerns are heightened and an investigation is needed.

5

5. The investigation

A Child Protection investigation usually involves a social worker and a police officer working together. They will plan beforehand to whom they will talk and what they need to know. They will interview three groups of people:

Interview the child	Interview all other children in the family who also may have been abused	Interview parents, carers, adults connected with the child
If the child is able and willing to give an account of having been abused which could be the basis of a criminal prosecution of the abuser in court, then the child's interview is videotaped. The child should be interviewed without the alleged abuser being present.	This would include any other children who may have had contact with the abuser.	The interview of the alleged perpetrator of the abuse is carried out by the Police. On the basis of this, a decision is made by the Police whether there is a case for prosecution. If there is felt to be a case the file is passed to the Crown Prosecution Service (CPS), which decides whether the case will be prosecuted. This decision will hinge on the following:

- What the child has said together with the child's age and abilities.

- The evidence that backs up/ corroborates what the child has said.

- Whether the alleged perpetrator admits the offence.

- How likely the CPS feels it is that there will be a successful prosecution.

Then there are two options:

No prosecution   **Prosecution**

A criminal prosecution is one way to protect the abused child(ren) and other children by making the perpetrator take responsibility for what has been done to the child(ren) and face the consequences of the wrong doing. The outcome of a court case can be:

Not Guilty   **Guilty**
- prison
- probation order
- fine
- community service

Once a perpetrator is found guilty, that person is thereafter a **Schedule One Offender**. This means that the name of the person is on a central police record. This is a life long label for a convicted offender.

It also means that if the offender later wants to get a job with children then the record will be checked and he will not be able to get the job. If there are concerns about children with whom the offender has contact, the register will be checked and his history of offending known. Action can then be taken.

6. **The need for a medical**
   At this stage a decision is made on the basis of the information from the referrer, the agency checks, and what the child(ren) have had to say, about whether the child should have a medical. Depending on the age of the child, the consent of the child or young person will be sought. Medicals are useful for two reasons:

6.1 They can provide forensic evidence, such as semen or blood samples, which will make a criminal conviction more likely. They can assess medical evidence that may be consistent with the child's account, such as genital injuries, sexually transmitted diseases, and soreness. This can then be used to support the evidence of the child's statement in court.

6.2 A medical can provide a helpful context for a child to talk about any worries she/he might have about their body or health, either as a consequence of the abuse or generally. Sensitive medicals conducted by trained and experienced paediatricians/police surgeons can be therapeutic for some children. Some children are able to say more about what has happened to them in such a setting.

7. **The need for Child Protection**
   At the same time as a decision is made on the basis of the child(ren)'s statement about whether a medical is needed, a decision will be made about whether there is a need for legal intervention to protect the child. Social services departments believe that an abused child should if it is at all possible remain at home. However, if the abuser is in the home and will not leave and/or the child is met with family disbelief, then social services may have to seek legal intervention. The options are:

7.1 Ask a magistrate for an **Emergency Protection Order** because the child is in danger. This can last for eight days. It is only granted if there is the suspicion of immediate danger to the child.

7.2 To ask for a **Child Assessment Order***. This order can require the assessment of a child for a period of up to seven days if there is the suspicion of abuse and the parents themselves would not co-operate with such an assessment without an order being made.

---

* In Scotland, the orders available under the Children (Scotland) Act 1995 are:
  Child Protection Order (or Emergency Protection Order from a J.P.);
  Child Assessment Order;
  Exclusion Order (excludes the alleged abuser from the child's home).

8. The case conference
The Child Protection procedures usually lay down the time limit within which a case conference has to be called after an investigation has been started; eight working days is a common time limit. The first case conference called in an investigation of abuse is referred to as **the initial case conference**. This conference is a meeting with a chairperson independent from the others who attend. It is attended by professionals and some family members. It usually includes; social worker, teacher, police, psychologist/psychiatrist, doctor, the parents of the child, together with a friend or mentor, or advocate. The details of the discussions and decisions of the conference are written down by a clerk who is there solely for that purpose. The conference will discuss:

8.1 Registration
This is whether the name of the child will be placed on the **Child Protection Register**. The Register is a list of names of children who have been abused or who are at risk of being abused. The children's names are put on the Register under different categories, at risk or actual:
- physical abuse
- neglect
- sexual abuse
- emotional abuse

The conference may decide the child's name does not need to go on the Register if it is clear that the abuse has stopped, the perpetrator has no contact with the child, and the child is well cared for and protected.

8.2 Child Protection plan
This is a detailed plan of how the workers and the parents will proceed together to protect the child.

8.3 Allocation of Key Worker
If ongoing work is needed to protect the child and support the family, the conference will name a key worker who will then be responsible for ensuring the Child Protection plan is carried out.

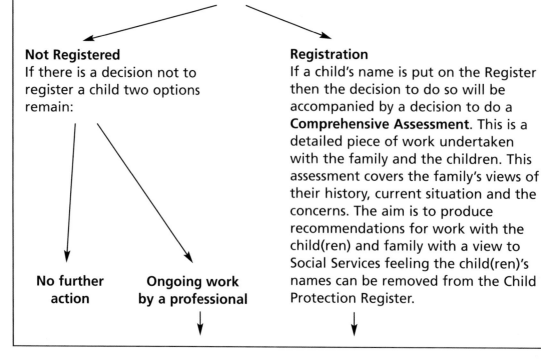

Not Registered
If there is a decision not to register a child two options remain:

No further action

Ongoing work by a professional

Registration
If a child's name is put on the Register then the decision to do so will be accompanied by a decision to do a **Comprehensive Assessment**. This is a detailed piece of work undertaken with the family and the children. This assessment covers the family's views of their history, current situation and the concerns. The aim is to produce recommendations for work with the child(ren) and family with a view to Social Services feeling the child(ren)'s names can be removed from the Child Protection Register.

↓ ↓

During ongoing work a Social Services department can offer help which it hopes will be taken up. In the event of a lack of co-operation by the child or family and additional concerns, legal intervention can be sought. This could be:
 a) Emergency Protection Order
 b) Child Assessment Order
 c) Supervision Order
 d) Care Order

If you are worried about the prospect of Social Services making a legal intervention in your life or if you want to know whether you can use an order to protect yourself or your children, get legal advice promptly. The Law Society recommend using a solicitor from:
 *Solicitor's Family Law Association
 PO Box 302
 Orpington BR6 8QX
 Tel: 01689 850227

They will be happy to send you a list of solicitors in your area who adhere to their code of practice.

At specified intervals of time after the initial case conference, there will be **Review Case Conferences**. The first Review conference will be held after three months and then at six monthly intervals thereafter. These are held to review the Child Protection plan of work, look at changes, and consider when to de-register the child.

*People who reside in Scotland have their own law centre, the address is:
 Scottish Child Law Centre
 Cranston House
 108 Argyle Street
 Glasgow G2 8BH
 Tel: 0141 226 3434

They have a network of around 400 solicitors who are familiar with aspects of family law. They also have personal knowledge of solicitors who deal specifically with child sexual abuse. The centre has two advice lines: an adult one (tel: 0141 226 3737, Tuesday to Friday); and a young people's advice line (tel: 0800 317500). These both offer legal advice and should the inquirer need counselling, they would be referred on.

The whole process of implementing the Child Protection procedures to protect children can be confusing to non-abusing parents and carers. It is for this reason that we have included some detail about how the procedures work. It is very important that you have some support throughout. Everyone's experiences with the agencies involved is different, it usually comes down to the individual professional dealing with the case. Often the more knowledge a worker has about the subject the more confident they are and therefore more likely to be able to talk without embarrassment. Chances are you will meet people you can relate to and people you can't. Mothers can find the ways different agencies approach the subject disturbing because the mother is forever having to slip into a different way of exchanging the information. One mother described it as follows:

The police were matter of fact, brusque and sometimes a bit coarse. Social workers were a bit softer in approach and talked of feelings. School teachers were gob-smacked, a bit cautious and sometimes seemed out of their depth.

Caroline

Hopefully you will find your key worker a great help. Not all mothers are assigned a key worker. It very much depends on the resources of your local authority, their policies and their present work load. Mothers who are not assigned a key worker will have to deal with the duty social worker. There will be limitations to what she or he can offer due to the limits of a professional's working week, other cases needing work, and the inevitable distance there must be between a parent and a Child Protection professional worker. It is best to establish additional support for yourself, from family members, friends, a voluntary organisation, such as Victim Support, or a self-help group. One self-help group facilitated by a Social Services department wrote the following handout on case conferences to help the mothers of sexually abused children by sharing experiences and making practical suggestions:

Didcot Safe Mothers' Group: our experiences in case conferences

Brenda recalls

- I was told there would only be a couple of people there, who would be discussing Helen and what's best for her. When we got there I was shocked, there were 13-15 people there. People I'd never met. Even the school matron was there. I hadn't realised they'd have to tell the school. I know now why, but I didn't know at the time.

- They decided they would put her name on the 'At Risk' Register. It was the end of the world for me. At the time I ran a playgroup. I couldn't understand why they'd done that. I know now that it was because they were not sure who the abuser was. I felt stupid and undermined.

- They asked me if she had any health problems and I said "no". Then the Chair looked at my doctor and said "has she", I thought "well why the fuck ask me?"

- I wish I'd kept the letters I got after the conference because it said Helen should have counselling. They've never provided that.

- I remember a nurse telling me that it's not always a good thing that they've taken her name off the Register because they won't follow up on what they said had to be done. This has turned out to be true.

- Things were brought up about my husband's past that I didn't know. I think he should have been notified that this would be done, so he had the chance to tell me himself first.

Sheila recalls

- The first conference I went to, my Health Visitor said it was her first conference and it would be an experience for her. I thought everyone there would have experienced conferences before. Her saying this didn't make me feel confident at all.

- When we got there, and went into the room, I was amazed at the size of the table. I thought I hope they don't fill all these chairs. They did.

- They told me where to sit. It was disturbing because it was opposite my husband, who had abused my children. I wasn't within kicking distance which was a pity.

→

- We had to introduce ourselves and I was asked to go first. I messed it up. I couldn't say my name and who I was. That finished it, I didn't come in with much confidence but after that I felt really stupid.

- I could feel they had power and I had none.

- They asked me if I minded going out of the conference and waiting in a room with my husband. When I pulled a face, they said, "perhaps we could find you a room on your own". I felt because they made such a song and dance about finding a room, I felt I had to say I'd sit in the same room as him. It was terrible. They brought us both coffee, that made it a strain to sit there drinking coffee.

Cecilia recalls

- My social worker came to the house and told me exactly what would happen, who would be there and that I could take a friend. I took a friend and a solicitor.

- The Chairperson was all right. She came to see me before the conference and explained things, that was helpful. It made me feel more at ease.

- I didn't know all the people. A teacher was there who would be her headteacher when she moved to secondary school.

- They said they were going to put Kerry on the Register, I was pleased. I don't know why. I felt it safe-guarded her.

- It felt like a safety net for Kerry. If he'd tried to injure her, the hospital would have her name on a list and would know.

- The people in the conference were gentle.

- I think I felt positive about the experience because I believed my daughter and my social worker were a hundred percent behind me.

Judy recalls

- The Headmistress of the school took me. I couldn't have got there otherwise.

- I had people I knew either side of me; when they saw I didn't understand, they asked for clarification. That was very helpful.

- It was difficult to keep track of what was happening. I felt everything was pushing in on me.

- I said what I thought they wanted to hear, because I was frightened to death they'd take my children away.

- I was pressurised to start divorce proceedings. I was told it would look better if I started the divorce.

- I felt I had to play ball.

- I'd been a playgroup worker and a registered childminder so I'd always been on the other side before. It was very difficult.

- No-one asked me how I was going to get home.

- No-one can blame you more than yourself. When someone says something about you, it confirms all the bad things you think about yourself.

Our ideas for mothers attending case conferences

- Once the abuse of your child has been disclosed or recognised, it will be useful if you can keep a file with letters sent to you. It may also be helpful to you to keep a diary/logbook of what your child says and does, and any concerns you have. You can refer to this at a case conference if you need to.

- The Child Protection procedures lay down the agenda items for a case conference. Ask for a copy of these well before the conference so you can know what will be discussed and prepare what you want to say.

- Your social worker will know who has been invited and from which agencies; ask for a list.

- You can take someone with you to the conference, a partner, friend or advocate. It's important to chose someone whom you can trust to come with you. If you want someone to go with you, you need to be aware that past details of family members may be discussed.

- If you are clear what you want to say to the conference, you can write it down beforehand and ask your social worker to make copies for everyone attending the conference.

- Think who you would like to have sit either side of you. Ask your social worker to make this possible for you.

- It is common for parents to find attending a case conference a new, confusing and sometimes anxiety-provoking experience. It can help to make a list beforehand of the points you want to make and take the list with you so you can refer to it in the conference.

- The case conference discussion may be complex; it is a good idea to take a pen and pad of paper to make notes for yourself.

- It might help to be seated and settled in the conference room before everyone else arrives.

- Ask your social worker beforehand if the chairperson could ask those present to introduce themselves first, before you are introduced/introduce yourself. Discuss with your social worker whether you want to introduce yourself or be introduced.

- Once you are in the conference, it can be hard to remember who is who. One way to remember is to make a plan of the table and write on it the names of the people and the agencies they represent against where they are sitting round the table. This will help you remember who is who.

- The chairperson will try to ensure that you understand what is said at the conference. If you don't understand something, it's important to say so or ask the person with you to say so.

- Remember that professionals are people with a job to do. They should be able to explain why they do what they do. They may be the experts about agency procedures but you are the expert about your child.

- Have a discussion with your social worker or the person you chose to take with you, about what you want to do after the conference. You may want to talk to someone in particular, or to have a cup of tea, or to go straight home.

- Make arrangements for how you will get home; ask for help with this if you need transport.

Didcot Safe Mothers Group handout   March 1994

Issues around prosecution

If the Crown Prosecution Service does decide that there should be a prosecution of the person who abused your child(ren), this will take time and take its toll on you all. You will need good information, advice and support all the way through the proceedings. There is a Child Witness Pack available from NSPCC National Centre, 42 Curtain Road, London EC2A 3NH. The pack has been developed by Government and voluntary organisations to help prepare young people and their carers for court.

While some aspects of the court procedures have changed recently we have included this account of a prosecution case by a mother. The issues and feelings she raises are invaluable and by inclusion we want to pay tribute to her strength.

Going to court: prosecution

From the outset I was under no illusion that it was going to be easy to go through with a prosecution against my husband. All I had in mind at the time was the emotional difficulty of co-operating to bring charges against a man I had lived with so long and with whom I had had four children. It was only later that I had to come to terms with the cold unsympathetic legal system.

In the beginning there was a flurry of activity – evidence to be gathered, medicals, statements, trying to locate my husband so that he could be charged. All done in a hectic week with the children and I left only in what we stood up in and relocated to temporary hotel accommodation with cooking facilities but no pots, pans, cutlery, no night-clothes, no friends around. Then from being the centre of attention one week, it seemed we were forgotten about the next.

We had been warned that because of the case load it was unlikely that we would reach the committal stage at the Magistrates Court for at least six months. In fact it was nearly eight months before that happened. Most people think that an old-style committal is worse than the High Court but you do at least know that this is not the 'real thing'; and that all the Magistrates need to be satisfied about is that there is sufficient evidence for the case to be forwarded to the High Court. Our case was heard in the smallest court room, one which is normally used for juvenile cases. I understand this was so that the public would not think of coming to watch the case – the public cannot be excluded but the Court officials do try to avoid inviting spectators. We did have some spectators – a group of young police cadets doing their day at court observing proceedings. They were a tower of strength. Inside the court room he stood less than two yards away from me while I gave my evidence. I had to speak so slowly so that the clerk could write everything down in longhand. It seemed to go on for ever. But at least the Magistrates Court was all over in the one day without adjournments. Then we settled down to wait for High Court. No-one thought this would be before October at the earliest so we were totally unprepared for the summons we had in June. We were told one evening at 6.00 p.m. that we had to be in court at 10.00 a.m. the next day.

→

No-one could tell me how many of my children were required so in the end we all went. To call it a shock is to underestimate – that night we were all in utter panic. It was adjourned. I must admit that I cannot remember now much about the next few weeks. I was so tense my blood pressure went sky high, my legs swelled to the point where some days I could hardly get my shoes on. We had more adjournments and days spent in legal wrangling while we sat outside in the waiting area not knowing what exactly was going on. In the end the defence barrister managed to get the case split in two – the charges brought in respect of my eldest daughter were to be heard separately from the charges in respect of my second daughter. And all this in the middle of the series of bus and tube strikes so each time we had to go to court we weren't sure how we were going to get there, never mind who was going to look after my three younger children.

As far as the legal system is concerned my daughter and I were simply witnesses. It was as if the case itself had little to do with us. To me my whole life was being ripped apart in court for public scrutiny. This was my first born baby I loved so much. This was the man with whom I had lived for most of the previous eighteen years. But the atmosphere in court, especially High Court, is deliberately dispassionate. The court room is cool, quiet and calm. The prosecution were not allowed to mention the abuse my two younger daughters had suffered, nor were they allowed to include the 'hearsay' evidence of two family friends who had been told what was happening. It is hard when you're asked oblique questions to see what the defence barrister is trying to show.

He was acquitted. The defence barrister – a woman – made my daughter and I look like a pair of scheming, vindictive bitches. The only salve to my conscience is that the jury found it so difficult to reach even a majority verdict. They took all day over their deliberations and in the end still did not reach a verdict on one of the charges – incest.

This was nearly a year ago now. It is hard coming to terms with his acquittal. I feel that when we needed society to stand on our side and vindicate us and condemn the abuser, they did not.

Another mother whose children were abused said to me recently that those who survive the experience become campaigners, and that is what I am becoming now. With the encouragement of our Borough Council's Social Services Department I have helped to start a self-help group for mothers of abused children. Talking to other mothers has been the way I have started getting my own experiences into some sort of proportion. If you were to come to one of our meetings the most glaring thing you would notice straight away is that out of the seven of us who meet regularly, in five cases there has been no prosecution at all. The other mother did have a successful prosecution, but only because the abuser, in this case the grandfather, pleaded guilty before trial to one specified instance of abuse. He got off with probation.

So if the police decide to bring charges and Crown Prosecution agree to go ahead, you are in a privileged position. Don't let my story put you off.

→

But do try to prepare yourself. Go to High Court and sit in the public gallery and see what the atmosphere is like. Ask about the statistics, in how many percentage of child abuse cases investigated by the Police are charges brought, in how many percentage of cases where the accused pleads not guilty at trial is a guilty verdict given. You will find the statistics chilling but at least you will begin to realise that should you – like me – be faced with coming to terms with a not guilty verdict it is not you or your children who are to blame for justice not being done.

Caroline

9. Criminal Injuries Compensation claims

So far, the consequences of a child telling have been described as: no action taken, a prosecution, and Child Protection procedures being followed. There is a further option which can be helpful to abused children.

Criminal Injuries Compensation

Children who are the victims of crimes of violence, either physical or sexual assaults, may be entitled to make a claim for compensation from the Criminal Injuries Compensation Board (CICB). The Board was set up to assess and offer financial compensation to the victims of violent crime, who have been injured as a result of the crime. The injuries may be physical or psychological. So children who have been sexually assaulted by strangers or by people they know – either from within or outside their families, can make a claim.

Claims can be made if the following applies:

9.1 **There is evidence that a crime has been committed**
The crime needs to have been reported to the police either just after it was committed or as soon as the victim is able to tell the police. When a claim is made, the Board will check with the police, asking for police reports and evidence. The Board will ask the police if the officer(s) involved were convinced that abuse had taken place and believe the reports of the offence are genuine. Obviously the best evidence that the child has been assaulted is a criminal conviction of the offender. However, the Board does not insist that there has been a criminal conviction. This reflects the fact that most people are injured as the result of violent crime, often by perpetrators who are never apprehended or by perpetrators against whom a criminal prosecution cannot be made. Such instances constitute the majority of sexual crimes against children. So while a criminal conviction is the best evidence a crime has been committed, it is not a requirement before making a claim. The Board needs to be satisfied that a crime of violence has occurred.

9.2 **There is evidence of injury as a result of the crime**
The compensation is assessed on the basis of evidence of injury as a result of the crime.

All physical injuries must be supported by medical reports. So if the child was examined when she/he was able to tell, the results of a medical will be requested by the Board. The child's past medical history may well contain details, which viewed with hindsight, could further show possible effects of abuse, for example, a young child with repeated urinary infections and genital soreness. While this is not evidence of abuse, such a medical history might be seen as significant if there was also medical evidence of abuse on examination at the time the child was able to tell. Any injuries incurred during the abuse should, if the victim can, be reported to a doctor.

Sexual assaults do not always mean that the victim is physically injured. Sexual offences can cause psychological injury. The Board will accept claims which are based on reports of psychological injury, if the assessment of the injury is supported by reports from the appropriate professionals, such as psychiatrists, psychologists, therapists. The professional report will need to detail what treatment may be needed and give a view as to the impact of the abuse and the need for treatment over time.

In some circumstances, the Board will consider claims on the basis of the psychological harm caused to children who are witnesses of an offence of violence. If it can be evidenced that a child witnessed a crime of violence and has had emotional difficulties as a consequence, then the Board can make an award of compensation.

There are other aspects of making a claim for compensation:

a) Claims can be made by filling in the relevant form. Forms and notes of guidance for completing the form can be obtained from:

Criminal Injuries Compensation Board
Morley House
26-30 Holborn Viaduct
LONDON EC1A 2JQ
Tel: 0171-842 6800

Claims can be made on behalf of children by a parent or guardian, a relative, or by a concerned individual, such as the child's social worker. Claims are considered by a single Board member who is either a judge or a barrister, on the basis of the form and reports from professionals involved. Neither the child nor his/her family is required to be present when the claim is considered. If the claim is accepted then the Board member decides on a level of award for compensation and an offer is made in writing to the person who signed the claim on behalf of the child. There is a right to appeal about decisions made by the Board. Presently there is a considerable waiting list for appeals to be heard. Appeals go before a Board consisting of either 2 or 3 Board members, again either judges or senior barristers. Witnesses can be called at appeals. If your claim goes to appeal we would suggest you seek legal advice; legal fees are usually paid out of the award (see earlier notes about choosing a solicitor). In making an appeal, you need to understand that the Board can decide to increase or decrease the original award. Whatever decision is made, is final.

b) There is a time limit for making claims after the crime has been committed. The time limit is three years. The Board is able to exercise discretion and allow claims, which have been made out of time, to go ahead. This discretion is quite frequently exercised with regard to claims made on behalf of children, as the Board recognises that delays in reporting sexual assaults and in making claims, may be due to lack of information, fear of reprisals or great emotional upset. When a late claim is made, it should be accompanied by an explanation for the delay. The decision of the Chairperson to allow discretion about a claim made out of time is final.

c)   The payment of an award to a child under 18 years will be to the parent(s) for the sole benefit of the child about whom the claim was made. The decision to do this will be made on the basis of the family circumstances, the age of the child, and the sum of money involved. If the award is large or if it is thought that the interests of the child need protection then the money is deposited and invested until the child reaches 18 years. The money awarded is held in trust for a child, interim payments can be made on request. Such requests may be for expenditure on holidays, special medical/psychiatric treatment etc..

d)   In deciding to accept a claim and make an award, the Board will seek to satisfy itself that the perpetrator of the assaults will in no way benefit, should an award be made. This is usually only an issue where there was a relationship between the offender and the victim prior to the offence. The Board will need information that the perpetrator is excluded from the child's home and that if there is any contact with the child, then that the contact is appropriately supervised.

Further information about making a claim for compensation on behalf of a child can be obtained from Victim Support Schemes, Citizens Advice Bureaux, or from solicitors (under the Legal Aid Scheme).

Making a claim for compensation can be very helpful to children as they cope with the consequences of their abuse. Children quite frequently feel guilty about being abused, about not being able to tell, and about the consequences of their telling or the recognition of their abuse. The process of making the claim and being made an offer of compensation can be helpful in that it can emphasise that they were the victims of a crime and are being recognised as such. While the money will in no way compensate for the dreadful harm that has been done to them, it could be the means to opportunities for rebuilding their lives and moving on. One young woman used the money to support herself during her studies for a professional qualification, which was a major way for her to feel positive about herself and independent in the future.

If a claim is discussed with a child, it is important that the discussions help the child to cope with the eventual decision of the Board. Children who know claims are being made, will need a lot of help to cope with either the claim being turned down or an eventual award of compensation. Parents/care givers need to help the child cope with whatever is the outcome. This should include thinking about how the fact of the claim is explained and discussed with other children in the family. One mother wrote the following when she learned that the compensation claim she had made on behalf of her daughter, had been successful:

It was the excitement on Helen's face, her first words were, "They believe me."

It was seeing my daughter happy and smiling, hearing her plan something positive for herself and good things for her future.

It was hearing someone say we do believe in and understand the long term pain and suffering of abuse.

Brenda

Chapter 5
And then what?

Help for you as a mother is help for your children too

The parents of children who have been sexually assaulted have in a sense been assaulted too. Your view of yourself as a mother, your relationship with your children, your sense of family integrity and well-being, the relationship of your family to your wider family and community networks, and your faith in others; have all been assaulted. Mothers of sexually abused children can feel physically inhibited; this is particularly relevant if the abuser was her partner or ex partner. The abuse can make mothers feel unclean and not want to touch others or be touched themselves. It can make them frightened to touch their children except in a very formal way. Mothers can also notice that others who become aware of the abuse can suddenly see the children in a different light and become insecure about touching them. It takes time for mothers to recover from the knowledge of what their children have been through. Some mothers feel the experiences of their children have removed them to such an extent that they are not 'theirs' any more. It is normal to feel in need of a lot of information, advice and support. A group of mothers of abused children who met regularly, made the following list of what mothers need after the abuse of their children has been recognised.

What mothers would benefit from when it becomes known that their children have been sexually assaulted

- A legal system that helps to protect children who have been sexually assaulted.

- Presently the law can be quite confusing and complex; it would be beneficial for those concerned if the law was easier to understand.

- Sometimes it is the mother and children or the children who have to leave the family home, rather than the abuser. This can cause more distress and could be avoided if the abuser left.

- If the women and children decide to leave the family home for safety reasons there should be 'safe houses' for them to go to.

- Women need a lot of advice when sexual assault has taken place, for example financial, welfare rights, legal and housing. Advice needs to be given in a calm, clear manner.

- There needs to be a choice of separate and/or together counselling for children and their mothers.

- Meeting other women who have had similar experiences can be beneficial and helpful.

→

- It is necessary to be believed and not to feel blamed and responsible for what the abuser has done.

- It is useful for the children not to have to repeat their experiences over and over again.

- If children are to be a witness in criminal proceedings they need to have preparation and support from an experienced worker. For mothers to help their children they too need to know and understand the court system.

- There should be available on-going support and assistance to help mothers over a long period of time, not only at the point of disclosure of sexual abuse.

- Mothers need support and advice when dealing with the consequences of abuse in their children's behaviour.

- Medicals for children should be sympathetic and 'child centred', with a choice of gender and ethnic group for the professionals. The surroundings the medical takes place in should also be pleasant.

- Resources for women and children who have experienced sexual violence should be well publicised.

- There should be facilities for children and babies in service agencies and public places.

- A free 24 hour telephone advice line for non-abusing parents and children would be useful in times of stress and difficulty.

- Police protection, if needed should be readily available and accessible for non-abusing parents and children.

- Specialist police teams in every locality should be available for example, police child protection teams and domestic violence teams.

- For mothers to be able to support and help their children after experiencing sexual assault they need to have information, resources and facilities such as those mentioned above.

by: **Pamela**
Ann
Caroline
Susan
Maria   January 1991

It is easy to see that many things the mothers say would be helpful are not available and this can be a distressing thought. The following list contains suggestion/ideas of people and organisations you can use to help you on your journey.

- Family

- Friends

- Helpline for mothers of abused children

- Helplines for general problems, Samaritans

- Your church

- Ask your social worker/health visitor if there are any groups you can join for mothers of abused children.

- Ask to meet another mother of abused children and talk to her.

- Child guidance clinic

- Social worker

- Rape Crisis centres

- Victim Support

It may be that you need help for yourself for any of the following reasons:

a) Sexual assaults on children can raise major dilemmas for parents/mothers. The agonies a mother goes through once she is aware that her child has been abused have to be experienced to be fully understood. A mother's sense of her own competence in terms of being a parent who can relate to her own child, can be completely undermined. A newly qualified social worker would not be judged experienced enough to handle a child sexual abuse case. Yet mothers are expected to handle it with no experience or training in the field whatsoever. All mothers need support. This should alleviate the danger that you may deal with these dilemmas in ways which are not advantageous for you, your children, and your families in the future. You need information and opportunities to air your feelings, if you are to be able to be available to your children in a way which will help them.

b) It can be the case when children are known to have been abused, that they are offered help to talk about and understand what has happened to them. When children begin to be able to talk more about their abuse, their thinking and feelings change and develop. It is really important that you are kept informed of the work done with your children and are offered opportunities to develop your own capacities to talk and think about what has happened. Then your abilities to understand and deal with the consequences of abuse will develop alongside those of your children and you will be much more able to respond appropriately to your children at home. Insist professionals keep you informed.

c) It may be that the abuse of your children has brought to the fore your own history of abuse. This is no indication that the two are linked by an inevitable cycle of abuse. Russell (1986) notes that 38% of adult women have incidents of sexual assault and harassment in their histories. The fact that you were sexually abused has not caused this to happen to your child. It may be that having been abused as a child or as a woman, has made you vulnerable. If the abuser of your child(ren) is/was your partner, then he may have recognised your vulnerability in the first instance and have taken advantage of this. Neither your vulnerability nor the abuse of your children is your fault. Both are the responsibilities of the perpetrators of the abuse. If you blame yourself, you detract from the blame that should be given to the perpetrators of abuse and you add to the burdens you have to carry with you as you walk away from abuse into the future.

Many women, who were themselves sexually abused as children, are able to recognise and respond to the signs that their children have been abused. They know how it feels and if they can build on that knowledge in ways which meet the needs of their children, then they probably have the most to offer.

d)   It may be that you need help because the impact of the abuse on your child(ren) has been such, that the behaviours are hard to understand and manage. What follows is a way of thinking about difficult behaviours shown by some abused children. We do not pretend that there are answers, just ways of thinking about and planning to manage behaviours which are more likely to help you to understand and to take helpful steps to manage your child(ren). Teachers often encounter problems managing difficult behaviours after abuse is known. If this is the case for your children, it might be useful to share the section on coping with the difficult behaviour of abused children with the teachers of your children.

What about you?

Very often after a disclosure a child's behaviour changes. They might display overt sexual activity either by publicly and/or excessively masturbating or by playing sexual 'games' with their friends or care givers. If your child is masturbating in public, it helps to say that is a private thing to do and have a discussion about the things people do in private and the things they do in public, and why. Children can make a mother aware of the sexual activities they have been involved in by doing them to her. This can be a means of finding out what has happened. For mothers of young children this is very hard to ascertain. Although it may be initially shocking, for most people things are easier to deal with if they know exactly what happened. The situation can be very difficult to manage. Obviously it's very distasteful but it is coupled with the dilemma that the last thing the mother wants to do is to make the child feel worse about themselves. A low key approach which explains why the behaviour is not helpful to the child and others but which also reassures the child that she/he is loved, is the kind of approach to take.

The burden that falls on a mother of children who have been sexually abused can seem overwhelmingly difficult. We suggest you might find it easier to split time down into smaller lengths. Sometimes it's impossible to think in terms of getting through the day or even the next half hour; don't try, just get through the next five minutes, then the next and the next and so on.

One of the problems mothers have is the same as a mother with a new born baby, lack of sleep. Not only are you coping with your own anxiety, grief and disbelief which often manifests itself in physical upsets such as sleeplessness, lack of appetite, migraines, diarrhoea, etc., but you are coping with your child(ren)'s as well. A typical night might well be one child having nightmares and waking you so you take him/her into your bed. Then the other child wets their bed which you change and put him/her back, only to have them creep into your bed and then wet that.

Your child may not let you out of his/her sight and cling to you all day and all night long. They may behave appallingly to you, being physically and verbally abusive all day long.

What can you do?

Be yourself. Inevitably you will handle some situations well and some wrongly. Commend yourself when you get it right and try to analyse what you did and why it was successful. Try not to rebuke yourself when you get it wrong. Share your feelings, it's fine to cry, tell them why you are crying. It's fine to be angry, tell them why you are angry, express your feelings by describing how you feel, for example, "I feel so angry because of what he has done to you." "I feel broken inside." By expressing how you feel you will show by example that it's okay to voice feelings. Smashing things can be therapeutic especially if it is a shared experience.

> One of my children was particularly angry one day. Everywhere she went and everything she did was a message to me that she was absolutely hacked off. In the kitchen was her breakfast upside down on the table and in every room she had been in was a mess of some description. She came into the kitchen where I was, her mood as black as ink and in a half hearted way started throwing the crockery on the floor. I took the bowl out of her hand and said to her, "If you are angry and want to smash things you'll have to throw it with more force than that, you'll have to put a bit of beef behind it." I then threw the bowl down with all my strength and we watched it smash. I handed her endless bowls, cups, anything I wasn't very fond of, which she smashed on the floor. She felt better, she had gained my permission to be angry and I had managed to share her pain.
>
> Another helpful pursuit I have found to be useful is bread making. Pretending the dough is the perpetrator and thumping the living daylights out of it releases a lot of pent up aggression for mother and child(ren) alike and it is something you can do together. Make a large quantity of dough and split it into however many there are of you.
>
> **Marion**

Helping your child express their anger isn't easy. The expression of their anger can be devastatingly destructive to them, to you, to people you love, to your property and other peoples.

Mothers often have to cope with the worst their children can throw at them. They are checking constantly to see if another adult will become abusive. Being tested in a public place like a busy shopping area with a child behaving like a two year old having a tantrum or deliberately walking into the traffic while your arms are full of shopping and you have to keep an eye on your other children, can be murder; especially when you hear other shoppers openly and loudly discuss your situation and how badly you are coping with it. It is not uncommon to hear from all sorts of directions that what you should do is give the child a good smack as if everything would then suddenly blossom into perfection.

We believe that smacking for disturbed behaviour makes the situation worse. Their behaviour is disturbed because they have been abused. To deal with abused children by further abusing them is wrong. Equally you cannot let your child be abusive to you and those around them. Some behaviours have to be challenged. If this becomes too difficult, seek help from either a professional or from a self help group.

My children tested me by refusing to do anything I asked. I decided to let everything go except the most vital things. For weeks at bed time one of my children would react by refusing to go into the bath, refusing to put on her pyjamas, refusing to clean her teeth. I hadn't the strength to insist on the bath or the pyjamas or the teeth cleaning. I reserved my strength for insisting she went to bed, limiting it to just one confrontation.

I think I was 'lucky' in that normally only one of my children went in for total non co-operation which in itself left me totally dependent on the others behaving helpfully.

Marion

When this happens it can be helpful to try and make a space so you and the co-operative child can spend some time together; for example, going out for breakfast can be cheaper than for other meals and if you go early it is often quiet and you can talk.

Teachers in schools find it appallingly difficult to cope with more than one disturbed child in a class and they are not emotionally involved; they are probably getting an uninterrupted night's sleep and they have been professionally trained. So if you are finding it hard, it is to be expected. Try to get in as much help as you can, maybe someone from the local church would come and do the ironing, freeing you to spend more time with your children. Asking for help isn't easy especially when you are not in a position to explain why it is needed and you're exhausted anyway. If there is a source of help grab it, anything which puts you in a position to offer more of your time to be one-to-one, or one-to however many children you have, will contribute to the healing and gradually things will improve.

It isn't possible to make it up to the child. Even if there were a well meaning relative or friend saying to your child "Never mind, darling, I'll take you away to Disneyland, we'll have a wonderful time and you can forget all about what's happened," it won't help. The message the child would be receiving would be that some people are prepared to spend a lot of money to shut them up.

Although having a good time out with your children is important, to begin with just letting them talk, cook with you, paint their feelings, you paint yours, reading to them is more therapeutic. Quiet well ordered activities where smashed emotions can be gently eased out and examined are more important than expensive activities like fun fairs or the cinema where communication isn't possible.

In your efforts to help your children, do not neglect yourself. You are the person on whom they depend for their lives, their sanity, for love and for fun. Everything you do will be a model of what they can take up and do themselves.

- Try to get enough sleep. It is hard but you need it. If you can't get to sleep it might help to have a regular bedtime with a planned relaxing routine before. If you can't sleep, rest, listening to music, reading a book, keep a diary. Like a mother with a new baby, snatch sleep and opportunities to rest when you can.

- Eat regular and nutritious meals. It is not an indulgence, it is an investment in your future health and well-being which is a gift to your children. Over-eating or neglecting to eat, solves nothing and fails to provide any encouragement for your children to eat well.

- Keep a diary as often as you can. Write down what happens to you and exactly how you feel. Acknowledging how you feel is important. Though it may be hard to believe it now, one day you will find you have walked on and you will feel better. Your diary will have charted your journey and show you what strides you made.

- Keep a file and log of all the letters, phone calls, and appointments with professionals/agencies. This will be useful when you need to attend meetings, or make decisions. Record what your child tells you about what has happened, use his/her own words.

- Choose someone you can talk to and work out with that person what you can expect. This is so you don't worry about talking too much, telephoning at a wrong time, or repeating yourself. It is much better to have a regular time(s) to talk which is limited but consistently available for you, than to be plagued with worries about what the person thinks. If you do need someone to talk to at other times or in the middle of the night, have the numbers of 24 hour phone lines like the Samaritans in your file; that's what they are there for. They would rather you phoned than felt alone.

- Ask to meet other mothers of abused children. What you will have in common will be greater than your differences. Listen and talk to each other.

- Tell your children every day that you love them. Remember you will not always like what they do, don't expect too much of yourself by thinking you should always like them. When you do need to challenge them, make it clear to them it is their behaviour you don't like, not them as people.

- If you feel in need of medical support but don't want to rely on drugs like tranquillisers or sleeping pills, it is worth remembering there are alternative medicines, such as homeopathy. The best recommendation is from a friend who already uses an alternative practitioner. Organisations which represent practitioners can often send you a list of who is in your area. Many advertise in the Yellow Pages; your local Health Food shop may have contacts. Alternative practitioners may have something to offer you. Check they have qualifications and are affiliated to a recognised organisation. Although most alternative medicine isn't available on the NHS, some is and most practitioners operate a sliding scale of charges.

- If you feel in need of medical help and have symptoms about which you are worrying, do consult your doctor. Neglected symptoms don't go away, and you will do yourself and your children no good if you are ill.

The symptoms your body is expressing will probably be as a result of the stress you are under. No one can take the abuse away but the appropriate people and agencies can see you get the right advice and support.

Whether you go to your GP or an alternative practitioner you have a right to expect that:
- you are treated in a non-judgemental way;
- you feel empowered;
- you have confidence in their judgement and ability so together you can sort things out.

- Take each day, even each five minutes, as it comes. Don't expect too much of yourself and neither ignore the many times you will cope and do well.

- When there are people offering to help you, take up their offers in ways which will help you, rather than to please them. People often do want to help, but they make their offers either in vague terms such as "Let me know if there is anything I can do," or in specific ways such as "You need to get out more, I'll have the children." Neither is useful. It is hard to take up vague offers of help. Often if you try to, it is clear that the person is busy or they didn't mean the kind of help you need at the time. The specific offers of help are usually about other people telling you what you need and how those needs can/should be met. We suggest you sit down on your own and make a list of what would help you and/or the children cope. Make a list which is clear with a range of ways you could be helped. Then when someone makes any kind of an offer to help, you could show them the list and ask if they could help in any of the ways listed. Ideas could include:
  - Baby-sitting once a week.
  - Visiting you when the children are up and playing with the children, so you can get a job done you otherwise couldn't get done.
  - Doing your weekly shopping.
  - Visiting you when the children are in bed and asleep, so you can have someone to talk to on a regular basis.
  - Listening to you.
  - Accompanying you to case conferences, meetings, court dates.
  - Taking the children to school.
  - Buying you a small luxury item you would never get for yourself, a box of chocolates, flowers, bath oil.

- Mothers who cope with children who have been sexually abused can have their parenting skills stretched to their limits. Anything which improves your parenting skills may help:
  - It could be something as simple as attending assertion training. You may find it easier to raise the problems you are coping with at home in a women only course. Local Authority classes often include assertion training. It could also help in dealing with your Social Services department!
  - Organisations like Parent Link are designed to increase awareness and improve parenting skills. Although classes don't deal with sexual abuse specifically, nevertheless the skills that are learned can equip a parent with more ways of avoiding difficult situations or dealing more successfully with them.

    – One-to-one help for you with a psychologist/psychiatrist can be very beneficial, if they have time to give you and if they can see their role as supporting and empowering you. What can be particularly helpful is talking in detail about the behaviour problems you are coping with and discussing options for dealing with them.

- Think about trying to join (or start) a group for mothers of abused children. Support groups can offer an opportunity to share your thoughts and feelings with people in similar positions to you. Groups that work well offer invaluable support to their members. When seeking a support group you might want to bear in mind the following checklist:
  - Is it a pleasant environment? How visible will you feel attending the place? Are there refreshments provided or facilities for making refreshments?
  - How will I get there and then get home?
  - Is it an open or closed group? Is the duration of the group fixed-term or open-ended?
  - Has everyone in the group got equal status e.g., is the group controlled by a leader or is it facilitated or co-ordinated?
  - Is the group organised by the same team your case worker or the children's psychologist/psychiatrist is working with? If you feel safe with the people working with you this won't be a problem. If you don't and you feel anything you said in the group could be leaked back and held against you, you might well be in a position where you could feel very unsafe.
  - What is the content of the group? Is it a pre-planned programme of work or do group members set the agenda?
  - What are the rules of the group and why have they been established? Do you agree with them? Are there ways group members can review the rules?
  - It is crucial that there is a rule about confidentiality. What is it?
  - What records do the group workers keep of the group? Can you see the records?
  - Do you feel safe (this will obviously take time to realise)?

One group of women who were all mothers of abused children wrote the following about their experiences of being in a group.

Joining a group for mothers of sexually abused children

I had agoraphobia and my biggest problem was getting there. I rang up to say I was leaving home and someone came to meet me and walk me in.

I worried about meeting new people.

My need to talk to other mothers outweighed the problems of getting there.

The first time I came, I worried most of the time about getting home, not a lot sunk in.

I couldn't eat anything in the group the first week.

Judy

→

I thought I'm not going it's just a load of do gooders poking their nose in. A friend convinced me to go for a few weeks and that I had nothing to lose.

The social worker was late and I thought, this is fucking typical.

I met one of the workers and I instantly liked her. We chatted a lot about the group so that was a help.

I don't remember what was said. I think we were all sussing each other out.

First impressions were very important, if anyone had said you have to do something that would have been it and I wouldn't have come again.

I'm glad I came back the second week.

Some weeks it would have been easy not to come but I felt drawn to come.

It was the groupworkers who made the first week comfortable.

It was important to me to know what would happen to the information I might share in the group.

Brenda

It was difficult to join as others had been in the group some time.

I can't remember much about it.

I used to get car sick on the way home.

I couldn't eat in the group to start off with.

It became difficult to come to the group after about 3 – 4 weeks because I'd felt sick afterwards.

I worried about it being a strange place and strange people.

The journey was a long way. It was a nice surprise it wasn't in a place which was clinical.

Sheila

I only came to the group because I thought that was what Social Services wanted me to do.

The driver didn't know where she was going.

I was early and couldn't get in, I stood outside like a lemon and I thought I just want to go home.

Then all these friendly faces said hello and I thought this isn't so bad.

It was scary; when they went round sharing their news I thought, I can't do this, I don't know what to say.

One woman had a fit and another woman said, just leave her, she'll be all right. I was really bothered. I thought what uncaring cows.

I felt odd and out of place.

At that time, I didn't feel I belonged anywhere.

Everyone else seemed so confident.

It was bloody terrible. I came back the second time because I thought I must have dreamt it.

The second time I came, I was doing it for me and my children.

Sue

Being in a group for mothers of abused children has meant:

- A place where I can talk about anything.

- Somewhere to go where you don't have to explain yourself.

- Nobody says "There, there, never mind", and patronises you.

- Somewhere you know people will be up front.

- It's the only place within our lives where we can speak about what has happened, no holds barred.

- I get lots of support and advice.

- I have some people I can trust.

- Friends.

- It's a different friendship, it's deeper.

- It felt like the first time someone could see inside of me and it was okay. It has given us knowledge.

- It's the first time I met experts who treated me on a par. I knew what I wanted to do, but didn't know how to do it.

- It was good to have what I wanted to do, confirmed.

- The biggest thing we have learned is it is not our fault.

- Learning we could not have stopped it, was another big thing.

- It is the first time in twenty years I can be my own person.

- We have grown in the group.

- It has given me confidence in myself to call the shots and get what I want out of life.

- It has given me a voice.

- I feel I got my life back.

Didcot Safe Mother's Group
March 1995

Coping with the difficult behaviour of abused children

Coping with the difficult behaviour of abused children after the abuse is known, is a major concern for parents and teachers. Often there are common questions that arise, which it would be useful to highlight here:

1. It is so hard to understand why the child(ren) did not tell about the abuse sooner or when it began.

Children have all the reasons in the world not to tell about their abuse. If we examine these reasons (see Chapter 2), common themes emerge. These include:

- that children are too young to tell or unable to communicate about what is happening, perhaps because of a disability or because they do not have the words to tell.

- that children are too frightened to tell because of implicit or actual threats to them to keep silent; these threats may be directed towards them or towards people, animals, or things that they love.

- that children are so tricked and bribed by the abuser that they do not recognise the abuse as abuse, or that the abuser so skillfully provides something the child does not have, that the child's loyalty to the abuser is secured.

It is helpful to look in some detail at the reasons children give for not being able to tell as these can provide some insight for adults who care for abused children. Considering the reasons why children cannot tell has an obvious message for non-abusing parents, carers, or teachers. Often the reason why it is so hard to understand why the child(ren) did not tell about the abuse sooner or when it began, is because the silence of the children strikes at our view of ourselves as people who care for children. Parents are shocked by the disclosure of abuse into asking "What kind of a parent am I that I didn't know this was happening to my child?" and "What sort of mother am I that my children were not able to talk to me and be sure they would be believed?" Parents often feel guilty and blame themselves for not knowing the abuse was happening. The reality is that just as the children have reasons why they could not tell, the parents have many reasons why they could not have known at the time the abuse was happening. For example, the parents of a group of boys abused by a local paedophile who was also the local postman, found making a list of reasons why they couldn't have known at the time, helpful.

> ### Why parents may not know about the abuse at the time it is happening
>
> It is often the first question a parent asks him/herself: why didn't I know?
> Parents often feel guilty and blame themselves for not knowing. In fact there were many reasons why we couldn't have known:
> 1.   The abuser often undermines the parent – letting the kids have money.
> 2.   Parents trust the local postman.
> 3.   He knew everybody.
> 4.   He was friendly to people.
> 5.   He was 'nice'.
> 6.   Offered to help people.
>
> →

7.	Belief that sexual abuse happens to unsupervised children.	
8.	Parents not knowing he had so much spare time.	
9.	Trust people in uniform.	
10.	He targeted single parent mums.	
11.	Children threatened into silence.	
12.	Won't happen to me.	
13.	He was Father Christmas for a few years.	
14.	You think you have brought them up right and they won't do that.	
15.	Want to think the kids are safe.	
16.	Want to believe your children are telling the truth.	
17.	Believing anything rather than abuse.	
18.	The last thing anybody thinks about.	
19.	Society does not want to know.	
20.	Believing we will recognise an abuser.	
21.	Was investigated so that meant he was clear.	
22.	Not knowing what the warning signs of abuse are.	
23.	He talked about getting a woman.	

So it is possible to get some insight into why children can't tell about abuse and why it is so hard for non-abusing parents to know about the abuse at the time. What always helps is for parents, carers and teachers to talk about their feelings, if possible with others who have been in the same situation, or with a professional. It is important to realise that just as the children are not alone in their experiences, neither are parents. Getting some insight is an important first step to coping; feeling guilty and blaming yourself helps no-one.

2. Why do some children seem to behave more badly when the abuse becomes known and has been stopped?

While the abuse was happening and the children were made to keep silent, there are several reasons why parents, carers, and teachers may not be aware of the difficulties their children are having or presenting elsewhere, such as in school. It is worth considering these because they do go some way to explaining why some children seem to behave badly when the abuse has stopped.

i) There are some abused children for whom school provides such an oasis of normality separate from their experiences of abuse, that they want to be as much like their peers as they can. The opportunity to be the same for part of their daily lives becomes a means of coping with being abused and feeling different, perhaps feeling she/he is the only person in the world having to live with being sexually assaulted. So behaving as is expected, is for some children the way they survive. It is also an opportunity to exercise some control over themselves and the way they are seen by others which makes it possible for them to cope with the powerlessness of being abused. Once the abuse is recognised then the children can no longer feel they can be the same as their peers and their sense of control over how they are perceived is taken away from them. This can be a point at which children then break down. This may be because they have lost the coping strategy on which they had depended for so long or because they are so relieved at not having to pretend any more that everything is okay.

One mother wrote the following about her memories of school when she was a child being abused at home.

> When I was 4½ years old I started school which was bliss for me because I didn't have to stay outside all day in the cold, like I did at home, and people talked to me. There were things to play with, things to do, I didn't have to pretend that I wasn't there. I was a person ...
>
> So school was a completely different world and I thought those children that cried when brought to school were totally stupid because to me school was heaven.
>
> **Judy**

ii)   For parents and carers especially, but also for teachers, the fact of daily contact with a child can mean that the changes in a child due to being abused can seem to be quite gradual and less apparent. For example, personal hygiene, school attendance, behaviour at school, can gradually deteriorate such that it is less noticeable to the people most close to a child. It may well be that the approaches used by the abuser are deliberately planned to target the child and gradually increase the extent of the abuse, so that sudden and dramatic changes in the child's behaviour will not occur. The deterioration in the child's emotions and behaviour simply may not have been noticed until a specific incident triggers concerns or the child is able to tell about the abuse. Once the abuse is known the whole adult perspective on the child hopefully will change and the child's difficulties will be recognised and support offered. However, for the child, the decline in their capacity to cope may continue and will have other ramifications which increase the pressures on the child. For example, if a child has been failing to make progress in school work and is not able to read at a level commensurate with his/her peers, then the fact of not being able to read may set in motion other school problems such as behaviour difficulties, concentration problems, the way the child is viewed by peers and teachers, etc.. Children can then be trapped in a downward spiral whereby they do behave more badly. If the abuser is the father and has been removed from the family the children who weren't abused might feel resentful that their father is no longer with them, putting greater pressure on the abused child.

iii)   What is often so upsetting to non-abusing parents once the abuse of their child is known, is that many will have noticed problems and attributed the cause of these to other things. With the gift of hindsight, parents and carers blame themselves for not having thought that there was a possibility the child was being abused. It is important to be reminded of the decades when highly trained professionals – psychologists, psychiatrists, social workers, teachers – have found the explanation that difficult behaviour could be a signal of the distress caused by sexual abuse, an unthinkable idea. Sexual abuse remains the last explanation most professionals and parents can contemplate, because other explanations are so much easier to imagine and have less awful implications for the child and for those who thought they were caring well for the child. So it can be that the child was behaving badly but that this was attributed to other causes, such as a change of teacher, adolescence, marital disharmony, etc..

iv)   There are some features of the consequences of the recognition of the sexual abuse of a child, which contribute to the impression that the child is behaving more badly once the abuse is known. The first of these is the fact that once the abuse is known, local authority Child Protection guidelines require that parents and the professionals share information at a case conference and begin to work together. It is often at this stage that the full extent of the child's difficulties and the concerns about a child are realised. So a clearer picture of the child's adjustment in different situations can heighten adult concerns about the difficulties the child has.

v)   There is a second feature of the consequences of the recognition of the sexual abuse of a child which can contribute to the impression that the child is behaving more badly once the abuse is known; and that is that there is a context and explanation for whatever behaviour problems the child has. Adult anxieties are heightened by the knowledge that the child has been abused, so that the behavioural difficulties take on more significance and meaning. For example, an incident of stealing by a child who has no known history of being abused arouses fewer anxieties than a report at a case conference that an abused child has stolen. Parents often ask about the known short and long term effects of abuse and worry more about the behaviours of the child. All children encounter temporary setbacks and difficulties in their development. For example, adolescence is a difficult time for most young people and their parents. It will be so for children with histories of abuse. Often the way difficulties are handled is the most significant factor in whether they are temporary or not, rather than the cause.

Many children do behave more badly when the abuse becomes known and has been stopped; understanding why difficulties become more apparent at that point goes some way to being able to think calmly about the difficulties.

3. Why do some abused children hurt themselves or others when they have been so hurt by the abuse?

For many abused children the effects of being abused, sometimes compounded by the consequences of telling about the abuse, are such that they have major difficulties. Difficulties can include: not doing well at school; relationship problems; lawbreaking; eating problems; running away; feeling depressed etc.. These difficulties are not inevitable nor do all abused children present such problems. However, some do, and for the parents, carers, teachers of these children, it is often incomprehensible why some abused children hurt themselves or others when they have been so hurt by the abuse. There is no one answer; what follows is a series of ideas which will hopefully contribute to understanding the impact of abuse on children's behaviour.

i)   Why should abused children not hurt themselves or others? Children are by definition immature and dependent, and are often the victims of abuse because of this. Someone familiar to them has abused their trust and sexually assaulted them. The impact of this abuse on the feelings and behaviour of the children will be varied, but what is common is the hurt. When we realise this, that abused children have been hurt by someone they knew and trusted, then the fact that they go on to hurt others is understandable. It can be a way of defending oneself from further hurt or a way of asserting control after the powerlessness of being abused.

ii)   Behaviour problems which are the consequence of abuse can become an established part of a child's way of coping, and continue after the abuse through habit. Children who are being abused often try to tell about what is happening to them in a variety of ways. Often changes in behaviour signal the distress they feel. If those around a child do not know the child is being abused and the abuse goes on for a long time, many of the changes in behaviour become habits. For example the child who cannot concentrate in school because of his/her thoughts about the abuse that is happening, may begin to lose all interest in school. This then has 'knock-on' effects; the child will fail to make progress, fall behind the work of peers, find it hard to understand the work, and end up being labelled by staff and peers as a difficult uninterested child. It would then be hard when the abuse is known, for the child to break out of what is a downwards spiral.

iii)   Some children who have been abused feel let down and angry towards the non-abusing adults in their lives. Children have a view of adults as all-knowing and all powerful, a view which we as adults often reinforce – how many parents have said "I've got eyes in the back of my head...." or "I knew what you'd been up to...", etc.? Abused children often assume that the non-abusing adults in their lives do actually know what is happening to them. They consequently feel let down by those adults, and especially often angry towards their mum. Society has very high expectations of mothers; any time spent watching television commercials underlines an image of motherhood as loving, protective and ... perfect. Children are aware of this image and sometimes their anger towards their mums stems from this. It is so hard for a small child who is completely aware of the behaviour of an abuser, to understand that adults whom she/he is told 'always know best', in fact didn't know what the abuser was doing.

iv)   It is important to remember that not only does abuse affect children's behaviour, but the consequences of telling about the abuse can be so difficult that the effects on behaviour are compounded. Children who have lived with being abused develop their own individual ways of coping and surviving. While their coping strategies may not always be helpful to them, they are nevertheless a child's way of surviving. Children who have been abused are strong children who have kept it secret; often to protect the family, or the abuser, or significant adults in their lives, from the reality of the abuse and consequences of its discovery. They have often used up a greater amount of inner strength than was theirs to give. Like any person in that position they feel over stressed, ratty, and disinclined to co-operate with what other people want. Most are ill-prepared for the consequences of telling, which can include the involvement of the police, social services, a medical for the child, an interview of the child, possibly the removal of the abuser, the upset of non-abusing parents, the curiosity of peers, perhaps a move of house and a change of school. The consequences of telling can often underpin why some abused children didn't tell in the first place and why they hurt themselves or others once the abuse is known.

v)   Abused children often have a very poor self-image. They frequently believe they are the only person in the world to whom this has happened. They know they have been used. This is difficult for anyone to accept. Sadly they quite frequently conclude that it is their fault that it has happened. A small child faced with the puzzle of whether the abusing adult is bad or mad, or she/he is bad or mad, will often blame themselves. Children do this in a variety of ways; such as excusing the abuser by saying "he was drunk"..."he'd lost his job"..."my mum didn't like him", or blaming themselves – "I shouldn't have taken the sweets"..."I should have said no"..."I should have told sooner". This low self image can be a feature which can underpin abusing and self abusive behaviour by the children. If a child doesn't like him/herself then she/he is unlikely to expect others to do so, and see no gain or point in behaving well towards others.

vi)   For some abused children, especially adolescents, the pain of the abuse and the consequences of telling are too much to face. If they were to admit to themselves how badly hurt they are, then it would be difficult if not impossible to live with that knowledge. One way of coping with such pain is to lash out at others, often indiscriminately, and frequently this lashing out is at people to whom the child is most close. It is as if inflicting pain on others will take away some of the pain the child feels. Some children turn their hurt on themselves, in a range of self abusive behaviours, which can include eating disorders, running away, drink, drugs, promiscuity, self mutilation, suicide attempts. These are expressions of great hurt and poor self worth which are extremely dangerous for the child. One girl who cut her arms regularly said later "It was as if physical pain was better than emotional pain and I was in control of that."

It is unfortunate that some children who have been sexually abused can retain a self image of being a victim. With careful management this can gradually be overcome. Some children react by going to the other extreme and bully other children. Unfortunately children have an uncanny sense of knowing when one of their peer group is feeling weak and some children can be cruel to that child. Most schools recognise bullying as being harmful and act accordingly. If you suspect your child is being bullied talk to your child and then to a head teacher to try to find a solution. A child who has suffered abuse will have much greater reason to panic if they feel that those in charge haven't got control. They need to feel safe and to be able to build on their ability to trust people again.

Children who have been abused are all different; no two children will feel the same or react in the same way. However what is the same is that the abuse has been an abuse of trust and power by a familiar adult. This will have affected them. The children need a great deal of support to believe in themselves again and this may well include support to learn to build positive relationships with others.

4. How long will this difficult behaviour go on?

Once abuse is known, parents, carers, and teachers are anxious for the child 'to get over it'. Some parents in their anxiety, deny their children the opportunity to go over what happened. It is important to do this. One father opposed his son joining a group for abused boys, saying "talking about what happened would only remind him and the sooner he put it behind him the better." We are all a product of our history; people and events shape all of us and remain with us all our lives. We can all point to the death of a loved one which changed our view of life, or a teacher who inspired us to develop in a given way or who dealt with us so badly that we have always found his/her subject difficult. The same is so for abuse. As adults who care for children we might want them to forget about it so that they will feel better, but that tells us more about our inability to cope with the pain of the children we love. The experiences of being abused will be with the child all his/her life. Many abused children say that there is not a day passes that they don't think about what has happened; it alters everything, the way children view themselves and other people. So hopes that children will forget it, put it behind them, or move on, can become additional pressures. This is not to say that the difficult behaviour shown by a child will always continue. The point is rather that children who have been abused need time and support to talk about what has happened and to come to terms with it in their own time and way. Pressure to conform fails to recognise abused children's rights to feel hurt, let down and angry, and to express these feelings. The more we as adults are able to help abused children see that their feelings are legitimate, the more the children will be able to know their feelings and be at peace with them.

Parents often want to know how long will the child be affected and how will the child be affected. Will it be weeks, months, or years? There is no answer to this, except that the abuse has happened and will be a fact that shapes the child's life thereafter. All children are different. The impact of the abuse will depend on: the age/abilities of the child, (gender, class, ethnicity and disability); the nature of the abuse; the duration of the abuse; the tie between the abuser and the child; the level of belief and support that the child receives; whether there is a successful prosecution/compensation claim; whether the child gets appropriate treatment work; the level of support for those who care for the child, etc.. It is more realistic for those seeking to help a child after abuse to take a long term view. If a child has been sexually assaulted for 4 years by a trusted adult, it is likely to be at least 4 years and maybe longer before that child can begin to believe that it might not happen again; that she/he is not to blame, and that she/he is not powerless.

Mothers usually have to cope with disturbed behaviour; this will sometimes be very pronounced and sometimes just bubbling under the surface. Hopefully things will improve gradually but what often happens is that just as the mother feels some sort of normality is setting in, the child undergoes a change in either physical or mental development and the whole thing blows up again. This can often take the mother unawares and put the family under dreadful strain. We can only suggest you deal with it as and when it happens and ask or scream, if necessary, for the support you find you need. No one knows how a child will be affected or what to expect. The fact that your child is finding a means to express his/her grief, anger and confusion is a release, providing it is dealt with in a positive way. Quite simply it's better out than in. Suppressing such feelings helps no one.

What the children need is people who believe what has happened to them. They also need acceptance of them as people and to have their feelings about the abuse validated. They need to feel secure about the love, support, and understanding of those around them. Then, they need time.

5. How much of the difficult behaviour is a consequence of the abuse, or a child's age and stage of development?

No one can answer this question for a parent. The only answer can be that from once the abuse is known, difficult behaviour will be a consequence of the abuse and the child's age and stage of development. One sad thing is that the abuse will affect how the child sees him/herself and how others see the child. As described earlier, all children encounter problems and present difficult behaviours at stages in their development. These difficulties are often around events or stages which trigger problems for the child and/or the family. These events or stages can include: starting or changing schools, a new baby in the house, falling out with friends, illness, adolescence, and so on. As mentioned earlier, the ways difficulties are managed are the most significant factors in whether they are resolved to the child's advantage and well-being. The parents of a group of boys aged 8-13 years who were sexually assaulted by a local paedophile made the following list of the effects of the abuse on their sons.

The parents' views of the effects of the abuse

1. Stealing from shops.
2. Not wanting to sleep on his own.
3. Saying there is someone in the cupboard.
4. Nightmares.
5. Soiling himself.
6. Telling lies.
7. Secretive.
8. Trouble at school.
9. Behind with school work.
10. Seems to be being blamed a lot at school.
11. Frightened at night on his own.
12. Being rude – saying dirty things.
13. Wanting to stay up late.
14. Swearing.
15. Having to have a light on.

Faced with an abused child presenting behaviour problems, there are some basic guidelines which may help:

i) **Separating out which behaviours are negotiable and which are not.**
   Some of the behaviours which seem consequent on the abuse are negotiable and can be incorporated into the family routine in ways which can reassure the child. Using the above list as an example; not wanting to sleep on his own, saying there is someone in the cupboard, nightmares, frightened at night on his own, wanting to stay up late, and having to have a light on, are all

behaviours which can be met with care and understanding. Often if a child can feel that his or her fears are catered for and met with understanding then the child feels more reassured.

Other problem behaviours are not negotiable. These are ones which are only going to lead to children getting into downward spirals of trouble and unhappiness. Again using the above list as an example: stealing from shops, soiling himself, telling lies, secretive, trouble at school, behind with school work, seems to be blamed a lot at school, being rude – saying dirty things and swearing, are all behaviours which need adult intervention. Some problems will need the significant adults in a child's life to discuss and implement a consistent and helpful programme of support. So for example, much can be done if the parents and teachers of a child collaborate to discuss how best to help a child cope with: trouble at school, behind with school work, and seems to be being blamed a lot at school. It may be that additional help will need to be sought from other education support agencies, such as the Schools' Psychological Service, the Education Welfare Service, or Child Guidance. What is important is that adults involved want to help the child, understand the impact of abuse, work together, and are consistent. Each planned programme to help a child needs to be individually designed.

ii) **Having clear expectations of children's behaviour and consistent consequences for doing as expected and for not doing as expected.**
Where there are behaviours which are considered non-negotiable, then it is vital that adults caring for a child are extremely clear with the child what is expected of them. Using the above list as an example: a child would need to know that his/her parents would not accept stealing from shops and that any known incidents will be dealt with in a clear and consistent way. They would need to detail what the consequences of stealing would be and follow this through should an incident of stealing occur. An example of consequences could be:
a) No incident of stealing will be ignored.
b) The parents will ensure where possible all stolen items are returned to the owner.
c) Where items can't be returned (e.g. sweets that have been eaten or goods spoilt) the parents will ensure that a portion of the child's pocket money is used to reimburse the owner.
d) After a specified number of incidents of stealing, the parents will involve outside agencies such as the police, family social worker.

Taking another example, the behaviour of coming home on time after going out is a frequent problem with adolescents. Parents should first be clear what it is they expect, which could be:
– to know where the child is going;
– to know with whom the child is going;
– to know what the child is going to do;
– to know when the child is going to return and how.

It then follows that it is important to be clear what will happen if the child does or does not do as expected. For example, the consequences could be:

a) If you come in as you said and have been where you said, you can go out tomorrow (or stay up till ____ etc.)

b) If you don't go where you said or don't come back when you said, you will be grounded for the next 24 hours, except for school.

When a child is presenting difficult behaviour and the adults concerned are preoccupied with managing the child, the need for the child to have incentives to behave well can be overlooked. For example, a parent can be so busy dealing with a teenager who persistently stays out late, that most of their interactions are focusing on inappropriate behaviour. There needs to be some gain for children to behave. An example of an incentive might be: if you come home on time (or no later than half an hour after the time – to allow for missed buses and the odd lapse) during the week when there is school the next day, Sunday-Thursday, you can stay out much later till ____p.m. at the weekend, Friday and Saturday.

iii) **The consequences of behaviour should match the extent of the problem.**
It is important not to over react to misbehaviour, and to threaten consequences which far outweigh what the child has done. So developing the two examples being used: if a child steals then it is important that the child does not gain but also that the parent does not over react. So threatening a child she/he will be taken into care or prosecuted by the Police, offers no scope for the child to test a parent out and also probably commits a parent to a course of action which the parent can't control. If having done this, the child sees the parent doesn't follow this through or she/he isn't taken into care, then the child learns to ignore the adult. It is important not to threaten to use all a child's pocket money to repay an owner, as that would leave the child with no regular pocket money and even more tempted to steal what she/he wants, as there are no other ways of legitimately paying for it.

In the second example, if a child has lied about where she/he went or has come back late, it is better to have a limited punishment like being grounded for 24 hours, than to over react and hit him/her or take his/her pocket money for a week or ground the child for a week.

There are several reasons for this avoidance of over reaction. These include:
a) It is hard for parents to keep up a longer or bigger punishment.
b) It hampers the child being able to behave so that she/he can make amends sooner than the parents expected.
c) It can build up resentment which leaves the child feeling very punished and antagonistic towards the parents and so caring less what the parents think about them.
d) It could also drive the child to be more secretive and devious to avoid punishment.

iv) **It is important to be consistent.**
It is important that parents, carers and teachers treat the children consistently. Otherwise there can be no real clarity about what is expected of children and no predictable consequences for behaviour. This is particularly important for

children with histories of abuse who have been previously given very confusing messages by the abuser about what is expected of them. Without consistency it would be likely that a child could feel picked on by an adult who was not clear. So where the adults caring for a child agree that some behaviours are non negotiable, then there needs to be a consistency between them about what is expected of the child and what the consequence will be for doing as expected or not doing as expected. Children more easily accept limits put on them if they are reasonable ones and if all adults treat them in the same way. It is also important to be consistent over time, so that a child knows what to expect. Otherwise if the consequences for misbehaviour change over time, a child can become resentful and more difficult.

v) **Helping children to feel better about themselves.**
If you suspect that your child is taking responsibility for the abuse, impress on them it is not their fault; it is the abuser's fault and they were right to tell. Say it everyday for as long as is needed and in every conversation about the abuse. We believe this message cannot be overstated.

What is plain from listening to abused children is that they feel hurt and let down, and very bad about themselves. When they behave badly it is because they feel bad, that is then the time that they most need reassurance as well as clear expectations and consequences. It is important in setting limits and managing difficult behaviour to let the children know that the adults around them understand why they are being difficult and are able to make it clear that they disapprove of the specific behaviours rather than the child. The parent can say to the child "I don't like what you are doing" rather than "I don't like you when you do that." For example, in talking to a child about drinking alcohol, a parent/adult could say "I can understand why you might be drinking; to get excited, to feel better, or forget what has happened, but the effects don't last and getting drunk can only add to your problems. Is there anything I can do to help?" If the drinking or other misbehaviour is an entrenched and extreme problem, the parent could consider involving appropriate agencies for advice and then establishing a more manageable half-way strategy, such as agreeing to some drinking in certain settings with some back-up resource/supervision. Then the adult is not seen by the young person as aiming to stop the *behaviour* completely, which for the child might be a way of relaxing or escaping from difficulties, and which for the adult might be an otherwise impossible task.

Children who have been abused need continual reassurance and love. However bad the abuse has made them feel, they need to know that there are adults who do not see them as bad, who understand, value and love them.

One group of women who were all mothers of abused children made their list of how they had survived the abuse of their children in the hope it would help other mothers:

How have we as mothers survived the abuse of our children?

■ We don't want our children to be alone.

■ My mum wasn't there for me. I know I've been there for Helen. She can tell me and I'll believe and listen.

■ Being able to talk to this group.

■ Putting all my energy into getting help for them.

■ Knowing other people believed her.

■ The only alternative would be to end it all, I knew I had to go on and cope.

■ Knowing nothing else is worse than the abuse.

■ We know how we felt when we were abused as children, and we don't want our children to feel the same.

■ Believing the abuse of my child meant I had to deal with my own abuse. I resented the fact that she has someone to believe her and I didn't.

■ Have a good friend or find a person that you can talk to.

■ Feeling okay that I could feel hatred.

■ Knowing I am not alone.

■ Realising there is no 'magic wand' and that how things go will be down to me.

■ Realising that while I always love my daughter, that I don't always like her and that is okay.

■ The children kept me going – they were my reason for keeping going.

■ Realising I need something for myself so my children don't feel held back by worrying that I've got nothing apart from them.

■ Learning to accept that we try to do everything perfectly and that we can't do that. The one thing we never wanted to happen, has happened and accepting that will be there all their lives.

■ Good weather and sunshine.

■ Being angry.

By: Brenda   Sheila
**   Judy   Cecilia**

The Didcot Safe Mothers' Group
May 1994

Chapter 6
Help for your child

The only way the child can start to release their pain is to be believed. In the same way adults surrounding the mother can find it hard to believe what has happened; many people in our society can't cope with the knowledge that children are sexually abused. Some people just pretend it doesn't happen and some try to rationalise it by saying it was just an adult being affectionate towards a child.

Situations can arise where family and friends either can't accept the situation at all or can only accept so much of it. For example, they might say "They could have dreamt that." What they are doing is finding some aspects of the abuse too difficult to cope with, so they make up an excuse or a different scenario. This can be very painful for the mother. The mother has had to cope with accepting the lot, and the child has actually had to cope with the experience.

Inform your children of what is happening

If your children are very young when they disclose they won't be in a position to make informed decisions about a course of action. However, to do things without informing them can increase their feelings of powerlessness. It might be that the best way forward is for you to make the decision and then discuss with them what decision has been made, why it has been made and what is going to happen. If your children are older you might want to include them in discussions to work out what to do.

The sort of problem that often arises is that, as a result of the abuse, your child is experiencing social and academic difficulties at school. You feel it would be helpful if a member of staff were informed about the abuse; your child is adamant they shouldn't be. What do you do? It may be necessary for your to override your child's wishes. If you do, inform your child of your decision and why you have overridden their wishes; that way they may 'hate you' for a limited period but they know they can trust you to tell them the truth. Their experience of trusting adults has been betrayed and violated. It isn't easy re-establishing the boundaries for them to push against.

In the same way, it's more honest not to cover things up. For example, if your child walks in on an adult conversation concerning the abuse and asks you what you are talking about, try to explain. That way it won't appear to be a discussion of a shameful experience. It can be hard for other adults to accept this. People want to protect children. It is easy for people to criticise a mother for informing and explaining things to her child; probably the usual explanation for the criticism is their embarrassment. What people have to understand is that sexually abused children have already lost their innocence and you cannot now protect them from that loss. One has to ask, "Who is being protected here, the child or the adult?" To join in with a pretence of their innocence is negating the child's experience of life.

We suggest one of the things you do after your child discloses is to make a list of the safe people they can talk to about what has happened. It could be empowering for your child to look at who needs to know everything; for example, the police and social services. Also, there are groups of people who can better support your child if they know something; for example, teachers and immediate family. Finally, there are people who you and your child choose whether to tell and how much to tell them. Your child may want to tell their best friend and other members of their peer group, of course, a lot depends on the age of your child. Discuss with your child the consequences of telling people, and the pressure they are then under if they are bound to secrecy, the consequences of them divulging and whether the information could then be used against them by, for example, bullying. This is where it is so helpful for your child to be in contact with other sexually abused children.

Useful words

Wrong: a good word to use is the word wrong, not bad or wicked but wrong. Young children tend to see things in black and white, good or bad. There are people who get mixed up in these cases like grandparents who may defend and protect their abusing sons. Probably up to the point of disclosure they have been model grandparents, so to describe them as bad negates all their previous love and input, but to say they are wrong is accurate.

How: another useful word is the word how. Your child(ren) might express a desire to see the abuser or someone involved in the collusion especially if he is a close relative. You can then tell your child that you understand their desire to see that person and you and the other people working with you, e.g. the psychologist/psychiatrist/case worker will work together to see how it can be arranged. Using the words 'if' or 'when' could be misleading but 'how' is accurate.

If the abuser is the child's father or step father

If the abuser is the child's father or step father it is more likely for the children to see the perpetrator as being both good and bad. Ideally what they want is for them to become all good.

Your child could accuse you of punishing them by not letting them see the abuser thereby re-affirming to themselves that they and not the abuser are responsible for the abuse. It might be appropriate to stress that it is him who is not allowed to see them, not the children who are not allowed to see him.

For any mother surviving on Social Security, trying to make the best for her family, Christmas or a birthday can be a nightmare. It's perhaps easier with small children who are unaware of the monetary value of things but when the child gets older and the designer trainers or a mountain bike become a must, the mother's sense of not being able to provide can be heightened. Very often the bread winner is gone and this can be coupled with the paternal relatives withdrawing and the children only receiving half the amount of presents they previously received. This in turn puts the mother under even greater pressure. There is no real solution and thinking of the number of people you know who have become emotionally damaged by not receiving designer trainers doesn't really help.

Why did I choose this man for my partner?

If your children have been sexually abused by your partner or ex partner you will probably be asking yourself why you chose such a man. The question is complex and we suggest it will probably help to talk to a trained counsellor or if you feel secure to bring the subject up in a support group for mothers of abused children.

It is sometimes helpful to remember that, given the role models of men and women in our society, maybe you didn't choose him, maybe he chose you.

A book which explores in some depth why certain people are attracted to others is *'Women Who Love Too Much'* by Robin Norwood, published by Arrow Books. The book isn't heavy and most women find it enjoyably informative.

List of everyday dos and a few don'ts

- Tell your child(ren) every day that you love them, say "I love you", rather than "Guess who loves you?" or any other similar question or statement.

- Believe your child(ren) when they talk about what has happened.

- Write down any disclosures as soon as possible after they have happened in the way the child said it. Keep agencies informed of developments.

- Let the instigation of conversation about the abuse come from them. If they want to talk about it be open to discussion; if they don't, honour that. Protect them from any prying inquisitions.

- Tell your child(ren) every day that they were right to tell you about the abuse and that it wasn't their fault it happened.

- Talk about people being 'wrong' rather than 'bad' or 'naughty'.

- Tell your children the truth about what is happening at all times. Don't lie to them to protect them; it can come back on you and you can then be seen as not honest and not to be trusted.

- Do only the necessary household tasks and spend as much time as possible talking with your children.

- With your children make a list of safe people they can talk to about the abuse. Talk about why the listed people will be safe to talk to and the consequences of talking to people you can't trust.

- Only make rules and set limits that can be implemented. Be kind and reasonable both to your children and yourself.

- Challenge anti-social behaviour by identifying what the behaviour is and specifying it is the behaviour you don't like and not the child, e.g. "I don't like spitting" rather than "I don't like you when you spit".

- Accept your child's right to be angry. It is the biggest healing factor.

Getting specialist help for your child

It may be that you feel that your child needs more help than you and the teachers can provide. You may need to ask your social worker what is available for your child(ren). Generally help for abused children is either offered as one-to-one therapy or in the form of a group programme of help. The choice may be limited and you may feel you have to take what is offered. It is beyond the scope of this book to detail all that could be available. However we want to give you some ideas which will help you think about what is offered and whether it will be helpful.

One-to-one work with abused children

The range of therapies available will probably depend on where you live, with the greatest range being available in London and the most limited range in remote rural settings. There is no one therapy that 'works' best for abused children. Much will depend on the quality of the therapist, the experiences of the child, the resources of the child to make use of the therapy, and the way the therapy is planned in relationship to the daily life of the child. If you and/or your social worker are planning to engage a therapist to do one-to-one work with your child(ren), the following framework gives some of the points about which you need to be clear before such work begins.

Engaging therapists to do individual work with children
A checklist offering guidelines for planning therapy

1. **Planning Therapy**

   1.1 The Child:
   - The needs of the child
   - Previous work done with the child
   - Statutory/Non-Statutory/Child Protection Register

   1.2 Types of therapy considered:
   - Play therapy
   - Art therapy
   - Psychotherapy
   - Family therapy
   - Group therapy
   - Drama therapy
   - Behaviour/cognitive therapy

   1.3 Therapy chosen:
   - Reasons why
   - Child view of therapy
   - Family view of therapy

   1.4 Choosing a therapist:
   - Qualifications
   - Gender
   - Ethnicity
   - Knowledge/experience of the problem area, e.g. child sexual abuse
   - Supervision of the therapist

   →

1.5 Transport:
- Mode
- Choice of driver and preparation
- Gender
- The need for an escort
- Pick up point/time
- Journey time
- Final return point/time
- Cost

1.6 Implications of the therapy for the child's network:
- Family and/or carers
- School professionals
- GP
- Ongoing work of the social worker

2. Contract of Work (Parties to the contract?)

2.1 Aims and objectives of therapy

2.2 Practical plans:
- Date therapy begins
- Duration of sessions
- Venue
- Time scale
- Cost per session
- Arrangements when child is ill
- Arrangements when therapist is ill
- Holiday arrangements

2.3 Confidentiality boundaries

2.4 How will the therapy be recorded/regularity of reports.

2.5 How is the therapy judged to be effective?

2.6 Criteria for termination of therapy

3. During Therapy

3.1 Communication from therapist after each session:
- What form?
- To whom?

3.2 Feedback from the child after each session – to whom?

3.3 Access to therapist between sessions for:
- Child
- Family
- School professionals
- Social worker
- Other

3.4 Therapist's feedback and/or attendance at case conferences/reviews

3.5 Support for primary carers.

3.6 Support for education professionals

→

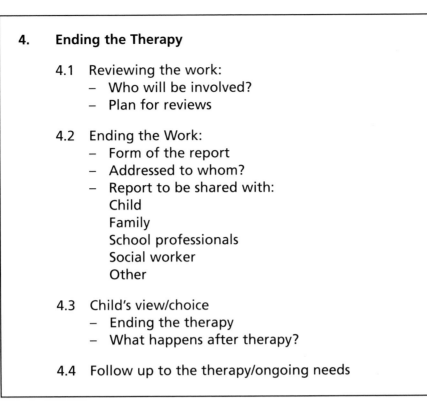

4. **Ending the Therapy**

   4.1 Reviewing the work:
       – Who will be involved?
       – Plan for reviews

   4.2 Ending the Work:
       – Form of the report
       – Addressed to whom?
       – Report to be shared with:
         Child
         Family
         School professionals
         Social worker
         Other

   4.3 Child's view/choice
       – Ending the therapy
       – What happens after therapy?

   4.4 Follow up to the therapy/ongoing needs

Groupwork for abused children

Abuse has usually involved isolating the child from peers and because of that many children who have been abused find group based programmes of help, less anxiety provoking and more reassuring. The benefits of group work can include:

Groupwork enables children to know they are not alone

Children who are included in a group of children who have been sexually abused gain therapeutic benefit from knowing that they are not alone and that there are other children who have had the same experiences. It is helpful if the composition of the group is such that each child is able to find another child in the group who shares an aspect of their abusive experience – for example, being molested by more than one person, being faced with rejection by the family, having siblings who were also abused, having had to give evidence in court, etc.. The reassurance offered by a group is particularly meaningful for children, who need an identifiable peer group.

Groups offer the scope to develop appropriate interpersonal skills

Sexually abused children are frequently isolated by their abuse, both within their family and from other children. Their feelings of self doubt and guilt set them apart from their peers and contribute to their isolation, as does their disturbing behaviour. The children are often trapped in a spiral of self-fulfilling prophecies. Abused children are unlikely to be able to alter mal-adaptive behaviour in treatment settings which do not offer the scope for practising interpersonal skills in a safe environment. Groupwork methods such as role play, problem solving, artwork, and discussions, can provide a flexible approach to developing such skills within the context of the peer group.

Groups lend themselves to the development of age-appropriate work

A developmental approach is important in treating children and families. Many of the groupwork techniques offer a basis for such an approach. For example, role play provides a wide range of age-appropriate options: assertion prevention work with toddlers; fantasy play acting of primary school age children; helping adolescents to learn about experiences found in peer group settings. The responses of individual children can provide the group worker with a tangible view of a child's stage of development, an expression of her/his feelings, and a basis for considering what other work needs to be planned. Some problems, of course, may be difficult to deal with in a groupwork setting – for example, issues of sexuality. Any treatment option is unlikely to meet all the needs of any one child and is not an end in itself.

Groupwork is often the most viable treatment option, when conditions for family work are not present

Family work demands a level of commitment from all concerned; in particular, the abuser (if involved in the work) must be willing to take responsibility for the abuse; there needs to be familial and professional belief, and there must be a motivation and capacity to change. Sadly, for many children who disclose, the conditions for family work are not present. Prosecutions are rare, and work to protect a child may well involve statutory measures and the child's removal from home. Whatever the circumstances, children need to be freed from being blamed or blaming themselves as a 'home breaker'. Groupwork can offer children a space separate from their families and/or caretakers in which they can vent their feelings. Groupwork can also serve as one way of monitoring children who are involved in family work and/or individual work.

Groups can offer children therapeutic confidentiality

The sexual abuse of children involves secrets between adults and children. Children often can't tell about sexual abuse because they may be too young to have the words to describe what has happened, they may have been threatened by real or implied force, or they may have been tricked by the abuser with talk of sharing secrets. Treatment options need to be considered in the light of the extent to which they provide an alternative to such a secretive situation. Family therapy often includes the use of video cameras, one-way screens, and live supervision. These conditions can continue to emphasise the power of adults to choose and the power of the family system, and can underline the powerlessness of children, isolated by the adult rules of confidentiality; this time in a treatment setting. Individual work can be experienced as a repetition of the secretive nature of the abusive situation, with the child once again involved with a powerful adult in a situation which has care-taking connotations. In contrast to both family therapy and individual work, groupwork offers a situation in which the children outnumber the adults and notions of confidentiality have to be discussed in a group of peers.

The inclusion of children in groups can empower children

In sexual abuse, adults abuse their power over children and children are isolated from other children. Groupwork provides children with a treatment setting in which they can develop a sense of the power of social groups. Groups can provide children with models of the real world in which they can safely practise taking turns to talk, sharing, making decisions, helping and being helped. Using groupwork alongside other forms of treatment can provide spaces and choices for children apart from their families which can increase children's sense of powerfulness as individuals and as members of a group. For example, being involved in making rules for the group can be therapeutic to children who have previously felt isolated from their peers and powerless.

Locally based groups can be a basis for future self-help

Groupwork brings children together to realise their shared experiences, and to develop their skills to relate to others and their capacity to help others and themselves. Treatment options offered by professionals are limited by being confined to the working week and to a given duration of time. Through groupwork children can learn about the resources they have within themselves and through their peers. The contacts children make in local groups offer scope for extending the range of help children can receive from and give to each other during the group and when the group ceases. Inclusion in a group can form a stepping stone to make contacts which are a means of taking control for themselves and changing their lives.

Whatever help you organise or are offered for your child(ren), don't lose sight of how central and important you are. Research into child sexual abuse is unanimous in one thing, which is that the single most important factor influencing how a child survives the experiences of being sexually assaulted by a known adult, is the presence of a believing and protective mother/carer.

Chapter 7

The prevention of sexual abuse

You may find it strange that we have included a section on the prevention of sexual abuse in a book for the mothers of children who have been abused. It is perhaps helpful if we say why we have done that before you move on to read about prevention. We have included this because:

1. The prevention of child sexual abuse is often talked about in social work and in schools. It is a misunderstood term and the mere mention of it may make you feel sad or that you should have prevented the abuse of your child(ren) or angry as you know you couldn't have prevented it. We think including some ideas about prevention will help you form your own ideas in ways which will be helpful to you and your child(ren).

2. It may be that your child(ren) will be included in the child sexual assault prevention programmes run in some schools. You may want to inform yourself and then check out the programme before you decide whether your child(ren) will join in the programme. If you do decide your child will do the programme you will need to understand about prevention and be able to prepare yourself and your child(ren) for the impact of the programme which will be different from that on non-abused children and families, given the experiences you have all had. You may think it best to discuss with your child(ren) whether they share their experience with the group and the problems that could develop from that. Children and adults alike do not share their pain unless they feel safe. It will probably be impossible to reach a decision beforehand as to whether or not your child wants to share his/her experience. It will, however, have helped to talk about it before the school runs the programme.

3. Sadly some children who have been abused are left so vulnerable that their vulnerability is seen by other abusers. It is helpful if abused children can be given the concepts and language of prevention to be more able to think and talk about the possibility of further abuse in the future. Obviously this needs to be done in ways which are sensitive to the experiences they have already had, which free them from the self-doubt and blame they have felt, and which empower them to speak in the future.

4. You may want to think about and plan your own ways of building child sexual assault prevention concepts into your daily life. In that way you can feel you are making a significant contribution to helping your children, those who have been abused and those who have not, be more safe in the future. There are ways you can do this which will help your children recognise abuse more clearly and be able to tell.

What does prevention mean?

In the face of mounting public and professional anxiety about child sexual abuse, prevention programmes have become one way of channelling anxiety. Despite the increasing interest in prevention work especially in schools, all too often little if any attention is given to defining what is meant by prevention, or to establishing how far any planned programme is able to address the issues as defined.

Prevention is a multi-faceted concept. It can be taken to have any one or several or all of the following meanings:

Stopping children being abused

No prevention programme can stop child sexual abuse. Prevention programmes can warn children of dangers, help them have strategies for dealing with approaches from adults, and encourage them to tell about such approaches. The most likely impact of such programmes in school is to encourage children to tell after the programme about approaches already being made to them, or that are made to them in the future. The statistics on child sexual abuse indicate that in any group of children, there may be a child who has already been abused. Programmes must therefore avoid presenting an over-simplified view of the pressures on children not to tell, this could lead to that child (and children who later face similar dangers) feeling adults don't understand how difficult their situations are and feeling guilty because they don't tell. Children tell when they are ready and feel safe to do so.

Stopping further abuse of children who have been abused

Unfortunately some of us have learnt by bitter experience that trusting someone close to us with our children isn't always safe. This experience will equip us not to place that trust in people again and to be on the look out for the tell tale signs that something isn't right. One of the saddest features of child sexual abuse is the fact that it leaves children needy and vulnerable to future abuse. A proportion of assaulted children are assaulted by more than one person at different times in their lives. An essential feature of any prevention work with such children would be to free them from their sense of self doubt, and work with them in ways which would make them less needy and vulnerable in the future. Much of such work is likely to be more effective if it takes place within the family or home base for the children. However, it is important to remember that assaulted children attend school and so may well be in a class which is involved in a programme of prevention.

Stopping siblings being molested

Case histories of children who have been abused often reveal that their siblings, both girls and boys, were also assaulted by the same adults. Much of the scope for prevention work with these children has to lie with agencies who have statutory child protection duties. Once children have been identified as at risk, there is often a great deal that a non-abusing parent, a nursery officer, or teacher, in daily contact with the child, can do to establish a warm supportive relationship with the child(ren). They can then begin to tackle informing siblings of the risks and teaching strategies for seeking help if need be.

Preventing generation repetition

It would be insulting to the large number of survivors of child sexual abuse to suggest that there is an inexorable cycle of abuse, whereby victims of child sexual abuse go on to be less capable and protective parents, or at worst abusers themselves. However, for some children the damage to their sense of self worth is so great that without help and support they will be prey to stresses in their adult lives, particularly in relationships. Women who have low self-worth are often sought out by men who cannot handle a relationship with an equal. The cycle of abuse needs to be addressed in all prevention work undertaken with children who have been abused, and with their siblings.

Better supervision of children by adults

The clearest and simplest way to make a significant contribution to the prevention of child sexual abuse is to improve the supervision of children by adults. Three examples illustrate this point. Firstly, how often do parents, having made arrangements for their child to join a local group (a choir, a sports club, a cub/brownie group, etc.), go to subsequent meetings to check on the group or ask their child "what did you do that was fun tonight?" and "was there anything that worried or upset you tonight?" Secondly, in a busy school routine it's all too easy to accept an explanation from an unfamiliar adult who comes to collect a child or from an adult about whom the child being collected shows signs of wariness. Thirdly, a common concern of parents and social workers is the planning and supervision of contact once abuse has been recognised. Issues about planning contact do raise anxieties about the quality of supervision of children. Frameworks for planning can be useful (see below). The point is that an increased level of vigilance by adults of children will contribute to the prevention of child abuse.

Better supervision of adults by adults

It is all too easy for most adults to consider themselves responsible only for their own behaviour. Given the prevalence of child sexual abuse, we preserve our naiveté about other adults at the expense of the safety of children. It would be quite wrong to see prevention programmes as necessarily involving direct work with children. Prevention programmes can involve adults – parents and professionals – increasing their vigilance of other adults.

Educating adults to spot warning signs of abuse in children

The pressures on children not to tell about abuse are many; changes in their behaviour are quite often the first signs of distress. If parents and professionals can be helped to spot warning signs of abuse, this could make a considerable contribution towards recognising that abuse is happening, making it possible for there to be effective intervention to protect the child and so preventing some of the effects of abuse. Nursery workers and teachers, who have daily contact with children, are uniquely placed to be alert to changes in children which may indicate they are being abused. In-service professional training for professionals can make a valuable contribution to this facet of prevention work.

Stopping perpetrators

It is helpful for non-abusing adults – parents, professionals and the general public – to realise that the responsibility for abuse lies with the perpetrator. No prevention work actually stops perpetrators. They are responsible for the harm they cause children. The field of 'treatment' for offenders has barely begun to tackle recidivism. It has been suggested that redressing the power imbalances between men and women in our society, and particularly the way in which boy children are socialised, will do much to contribute to lessening the violence of men towards women and children.

It is all too easy to reduce the concept of prevention to programmes of direct work with children in which the aim is to teach children about 'yes' and 'no' feelings, to learn to say 'no' to abusive adults, and to tell of such approaches. This section considers some of the issues involved in such work with children but also seeks to remind us all that such direct work is only one contribution that can be made to the prevention of child sexual abuse.

You might be interested to read a list of prevention strategies drawn up by a group of boys aged 8–13 years who had all been abused by the same paedophile:

Keeping safe

1. Crack them one.
2. Tell someone – The police
   – mum or dad
   – friends
   – teacher
   – ChildLine
   – NSPCC
   – National Helpline
   – Samaritans
   – Social Services.
3. Be wary of people, not trusting.
4. Not go in people's houses.
5. Always telling mum or dad where I am.
6. Not taking money, sweets, drinks or cigarettes from people without our parents' permission.
7. No matter what you have done you have the right to say no.
8. Find a safe time and a safe place to tell.
9. Telling a lie like, my mum said I've got to go home or she'll come to get me. She knows where I am.
10. Distract the person, escape and go for help.

Contact issues

A Criminal Court could deliver a not guilty verdict but the protection of a child under civil jurisdiction may still be needed. Therefore a not guilty verdict does not have to mean the perpetrator will be given unsupervised contact rights with his children.

If you are faced with the fact that your partner abused your children, there has been no prosecution or a failed prosecution, and he is demanding contact with the children, then the following checklist for considering planning contact after abuse has been recognised, could be useful. Our advice is to take this framework to a solicitor (contact the Solicitor's Family Law Association for a list of solicitors with child care experience) and ask the solicitor to help you decide whether you want this contact to take place, how to oppose it if you don't, and how to plan it if you do.

Ask the solicitor you are considering engaging what barrister she/he uses and ask questions about them. Do bear in mind if your solicitor is a man, has a male clerk, engages a male barrister who in turn has a male pupil, that you could be in a position of discussing more intimate details than you would normally discuss with your doctor with between one to four men.

If the abuser is asking for contact the choices are:

- Unsupervised contact

- Supervised contact

- No contact

Unsupervised contact

If the abuser is asking for unsupervised contact then this will need to be discussed with your case worker and solicitor and your feelings on the subject made clear. We hope that unsupervised contact given to sexual abusers is a thing of the past.

Supervised contact

In order for the healing process to begin and continue, the child has to be aware that she/he wasn't to blame in any way for what happened. This can be greatly enhanced if the perpetrator admits the abuse. There are three things he must do:

1. Admit it – say "I did it."

2. Take responsibility for the abuse – say "It was my fault."

3. Apologise – say "I'm sorry."

We believe that until the perpetrator has done these three things that supervised contact isn't in the best interests of the child. The question of what he is going to say when asked why he hasn't been able to see the child(ren) will have to be answered. If his answer avoids his taking responsibility for his absence then the way forward would seem blocked. It is unlikely that an abuser will take responsibility. Most abusers have a great deal invested in not admitting the abuse; for example, loss of employment, status or criminal prosecution. While the law seeks to protect children, it does little to encourage abusers to take responsibility for their actions. Should his answer avoid his taking responsibility for his absence, then you may feel that no contact is appropriate. Ultimately the court will decide who has access and what form it takes. They will take the wishes of all parties including the children's into consideration. If it is still considered in the children's best interests for supervised contact to go ahead, then the framework which follows may be useful.

We feel we should point out that sexual abusers are notoriously clever. It is possible for them to influence a child without the knowledge of the supervisor. For example, the abuser could say "I'm friends with Billy now." The supervisor would be completely unaware that Billy was a policeman, yet the child could construe from that information that the abuser was no longer being blamed. It is impossible to foresee every eventuality; supervised contact needs careful planning, the children and all caring parties should be happy with the arrangements and feel able to challenge them at any time.

No contact

If the perpetrator has been denied contact he may well ask if he can send birthday and Christmas cards to the child(ren). Should you decide that the sending of cards is permissible you may find the following guidelines useful:

- The cards will not contain anything (e.g. money).

- The cards must be sent to a different address to the child's home (e.g. the mother's solicitor).

- The mother reserves the right not to pass on the cards to the children.

- The cards will not be displayed but placed in a folder where the child(ren) can view them as and when they wish.

Should the court decide that receiving mail from the abuser is in the children's best interests and you feel it isn't, you will need to return to court with a clear and concise argument to attempt to get the order changed.

Considering planning contact after abuse has been recognised: a framework

The following framework sets out some ideas for thinking about planning contact. If the abuser of your child is asking for contact, you can use this framework as a basis for discussing your concerns with your social worker or with your solicitor.

General issues

1. The presumption in the Children Act is that children should have contact with their parents. However, what the Act states is that the welfare of child(ren) is paramount.

2. The Children Act requires that planning, both immediate and long term, should take place as soon as a child enters care.

3. Consideration needs to be given to the basis on which contact would be judged to be helpful when a child has been abused. Social Workers are expected to make judgements on the basis of the Welfare Checklist. Ask to see this.

One way forward would be to consider the child/family circumstances which would contribute to the contact being more likely to be safe and less likely to be injurious.

Child

- Ascertain the wishes of the child. On what basis would a child say 'no'? Does the work make it equally possible for the child to say 'yes' or 'no' to contact? Are the techniques of work with the child appropriate in terms of the child:

- age/developmental stage
- gender
- abilities/disabilities
- race/culture/religion
- temperament
- history of the child
- ongoing support for the child

- by whom will this be done?
- in what context will the child be asked?
- how worded?

- Purpose of the contact. How far is that congruent with the protection of the child and the overall plans for the child? The possibility of contact needs to be separately considered with respect to:
  - the abuser with consideration of whether the abuser is:
    - suspected;
    - named;
    - proven.

  - mum
  - siblings
  - grandparents
  - extended family
  - previous carers
  - friends.

- Legal protection of the child needs to be assured.

- Family base of the child needs to be secure, helpful to the child, and able to cope with contact and the consequences of contact for the child.

- Treatment work on abuse with the child should have been planned and started.

- There is a planned system of monitoring the impact of the contact on the child using information from the supervision of the contact, the carers, the teacher(s) of the child and from the child.

Family

- Abuser has taken responsibility/been prosecuted.

- Mother has believed the child:
  - distinction should be made in contact arrangements between abusing/non-abusing parents given mum is separate from the abuser;
  - work being done with mum to help her develop her belief and support for her children.

- Siblings know what has happened:
  - interviewed in their own right;
  - on the Register if need be;
  - work has been done to put what has happened since disclosure in a positive frame round the child who has told.

- Prevention work undertaken with siblings.

- System for monitoring siblings which is ongoing in nursery/school and linked to any ongoing Child Protection Review system.

- When there is a history of domestic violence, consideration needs to be given to:
  - were the child(ren) physically assaulted?
  - if the children were witnesses – the emotional effects on them of violence and of any subsequent contact;
  - the possibility of violence recurring during the contact, towards the non-abusing parent and/or the child(ren).

Arranging contact

- Preparation and follow-up needs to be agreed in writing with **all** concerned *before* contact is arranged.

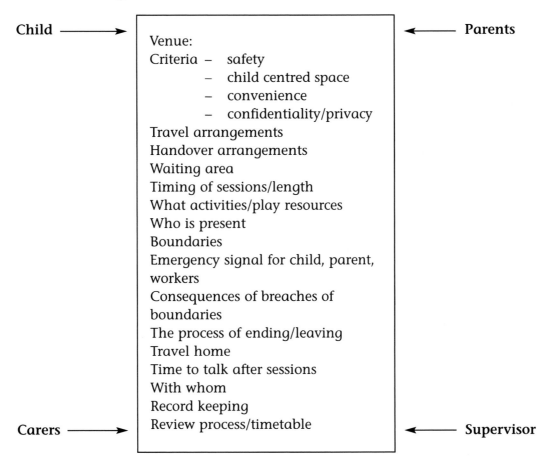

Child ⟶

Venue:
Criteria – safety
  – child centred space
  – convenience
  – confidentiality/privacy
Travel arrangements
Handover arrangements
Waiting area
Timing of sessions/length
What activities/play resources
Who is present
Boundaries
Emergency signal for child, parent, workers
Consequences of breaches of boundaries
The process of ending/leaving
Travel home
Time to talk after sessions
With whom
Record keeping
Review process/timetable

⟵ Parents

Carers ⟶

⟵ Supervisor

- Supervision of contact.
  - Can supervision be done by someone who was not part of the investigation?
  - Can supervision provide sufficient protection for children during contact?
  - Supervisors need to be:
    - knowledgeable with regard to child sexual abuse;
    - aware of context of contact;
    - have the confidence of the child;
    - clear about their role;
    - able to challenge;
    - significant in subsequent Child Protection Review/legal proceedings.

Prevention work by parents

This section is written to give you ideas about work you can do with young children who have been abused or with the young siblings of an abused child.

Parents can make the biggest contribution to the likelihood that their child will be less vulnerable to sexual assaults by known adults and/or be more able to tell about such an assault, should it happen. Unfortunately many parents do little work with their children to prevent abuse by known adults. It is interesting to consider why this is so. Three main reasons emerge:

Firstly, parents assume or hope that their child will not be sexually assaulted by anyone they know. This hope is based on a variety of mistaken assumptions which it might be useful to list:

   i)   *Child sexual abuse doesn't happen very often.* In fact, abuse by known adults happens to 1 in 20 of the population before the age of 15 years.

   ii) *Child sexual abuse is largely committed by strangers and as I supervise my child, it won't happen.* In fact, the majority of assaults on children are committed by adults known to the child or family beforehand.

   iii) *Child sexual abuse doesn't happen to children in families like mine.* In fact, there is no evidence that child sexual abuse happens to certain types of children or families. It is a sad event which cuts across geography, class, race, culture, ability/disabilities, and cannot be predicted on a basis of any of these factors.

Secondly, parents fear talking about the problem as they think it will undermine a child's capacity to trust and feel secure with family and friends. Parents mistakenly think that in order to warn their child about sexual assaults they should talk solely about the dangers. It is more positive to talk to children in ways which enhance their sense of self-esteem, their capacity to relate to others, and the likelihood they will be more safe.

Thirdly, if parents do want to talk to their children about child sexual abuse, they can find it hard to do so because they are unsure where to start, what words to use, and how to answer the difficult questions that small children are so good at asking. So often they say little or nothing for fear of getting it wrong. They postpone talking about it, thinking it will be easier when the child is older or if the teacher does it.

It is worth reminding ourselves that children learn what is speakable and unspeakable from what we as parents/adults do and say, and what we don't do and don't say. Children's ideas, language and behaviour all develop from the care and influence of their parents and other significant adults. There are a variety of ways we can as parents/carers carry out child sexual abuse prevention work with our children every single day.

1. Be informed about the nature of child sexual abuse

As parents/adults we are responsible for children in our care. Children are by definition, dependent, immature, and in need of our protection. If we are to protect children from possible dangers then we need to be informed about the nature of dangers to children. We can't help our children avoid dangers or minimise the effects of dangerous events, if we are not informed ourselves. So just as we need to know the dangers of water or electricity and how to rescue and revive our children in the event of an accident; so we need to know about the danger of child sexual abuse, the parameters of the problem, ways of reducing the likelihood it will happen, and ways of increasing the likelihood our children will tell us if it does happen.

2. Spend time every day listening to our children

Children talk a lot and it's all too easy for parents at home or for professionals who work with children, to think that they listen to the children in their care. Children are excited by the world and their experiences, and while they are young they are pre-occupied with their egocentric view of the world. They will often want to share their experiences in constant chatter with those around them. It is an irony that almost as soon as our children have begun to speak in a clear and fluent way, that we begin to curb this with the usual parent refrains, such as "don't interrupt" … "wait till I have finished speaking" … "don't talk while I am talking" and so on. This is not to say that parents shouldn't teach their children how to exchange conversation, and to respect the rights of others to have their say. However, what this needs to be tempered by, is a regular daily time when children know they can talk and be listened to. We think we do this, but we need to consider how often we do so, while we are doing something else or when children are in groups, with siblings, friends, classmates. Children need to understand that they can't always demand the undivided attention of an adult and they need to talk in groups; but they also need reliable times when they are listened to by an adult who is not pre-occupied and whose attention is not divided. If children know that they will be regularly listened to on an individual basis and what they say is patiently heard, then when they are worried and/or have had a frightening experience, they are more likely to feel confident that they could talk about this and that there will be a time when they can do this. Sometimes it's hard for us under the pressures of coping with the demands on us as parents or where there are more than one child's needs to meet, to make time. It is then all the more important to do so, if children are to have confidence that we will listen to them. Special listening time can be built into bathtimes, staggering bedtimes for siblings, having children help in turn with activities such as cooking or tidying, all of which create an opportunity for listening rather than being an end in themselves.

3. Listening and asking questions

The way we listen to children will affect their confidence to speak to us and the things they tell us. If we are preoccupied or ask children questions when there is little time to reply, then they will assume we don't want to hear what they say or that we only want to hear briefly. Take the example of school; how often do we as parents ask "How was school?" as we do something else, not look at the child, and accept the usual monosyllabic answers of "Fine", "Boring", "Can't remember". Often children don't want to talk about school when they get home because they are tired, or just want to relax or to keep school and home separate. Even in the face of this apparent disinclination to talk, it is still important for parents to signal their interest by asking questions and giving the opportunity to talk to their children. Simple questions such as "What was for lunch today?" … "Did you have one pudding or two puddings today?" … "Who did have two puddings?" … "What did you like most about school today?" … "What did you like least about school today?" Faced with no answers, parents can signal their understanding. "Guess you are too tired to talk now, maybe you'd tell me later, I'll ask you again at bedtime, I want to hear how things are for you." The fact that we take time, ask questions, and use questions to demonstrate that we want to hear about good and bad experiences, is helpful in letting a child know that we are conscious they face difficulties and we are prepared to listen to these.

4. Whenever possible giving children explanations and choices

One of the things we know is that people who sexually assault children do not give them real choices. A sexual assault on a child is an abuse of power over that child, denying them the most basic right which is to say who touches their body. Children who are sexually assaulted are either too young or unable to tell what is happening, or are threatened not to tell, or are tricked and bribed and may not even recognise the abuse as abusive. If we want to prevent our children being abused or enable them to tell if it happens, then the more we can provide our children with clear explanations of events around them and of our behaviour as parents, and offer them choices; then they are more likely to react to abusive behaviour in a way which can alert us. An example would be the way we as parents touch our children. We need to talk to children about what we are doing and why we are doing it. So even with a small baby, we can be saying, "Now we are going upstairs to change your nappy because you are wet, up we go, now you lie down, I'll take your trousers off so I can change your nappy, here comes the baby lotion ...." The message is clear that we are touching the child for a purpose and explaining. Wherever possible children should be given choices which indicate that their body is theirs and that they can choose who touches it, such as "Would you like to hold my hand?" and when the answer is no, we can demonstrate our acceptance of the decision. So children can decline to kiss grandpa or to be tickled by uncle, without the pressures that can so often be brought to bear, like "Don't be rude"... "You'll hurt his feelings"... "You won't get any sweets." Obviously there are times when children can't choose who touches them, like a four-year-old having to hold mummy's hand crossing a busy road or a child with a pain needing to be examined by a doctor. We need to give clear explanations when children can't choose about being touched, and continue to give them choices when they can. This way they can develop a sense that they deserve explanations and they have choices. If we were to handle our children roughly, with no explanations and choices, then the distinction between non-abusing and abusing adult behaviour will be less clear to them.

5. Avoid a punitive approach to mistakes and misbehaviour

Children who have been abused, will often blame themselves for what happened to them. They will say "I should have said no" ... "stopped him".... "I should have told".... "I thought I was the only person this has happened to" (implying there is something about me which explains why it happened). It is often because they partly blame themselves that they feel trapped by the abuser and unable to tell and get help. One group of boys who had been tricked by a paedophile into trusting him, accepted his bribes of sweets, money, cigarettes and alcohol. When he subsequently assaulted them, they felt unable to tell because their parents would be cross with them for going to his house, for smoking and drinking, for not telling sooner. They didn't understand the way he had bribed them and felt implicated in what subsequently happened. Parents need to be aware that the choices they make in terms of strategies for dealing with mistakes and misbehaviour will affect the trust their children have in them. Choices need to be made which leave children feeling confident they can make mistakes and be supported, and that their misbehaviour will be dealt with firmness and understanding, so that there is no need to lie or fear parents finding out. A punitive parental approach to mistakes and misbehaviours has the following effects:

- Firstly, it spoils the positive features of the parent-child relationship.

- Secondly, it doesn't offer guidance about how a child should behave.

- Thirdly, it provides an unhelpful model about what bigger, more powerful people do to children, which they will in their turn imitate.

- Fourthly, it provides the child with pressure to lie or deny what has happened to avoid the punishment.

So it is important to avoid a punitive approach to children's mistakes and misbehaviour so that they do not fear our reactions when they need help.

6. Talk openly to children about their bodies and sex in age appropriate ways

Children's interests and questions about their bodies, their parents' bodies, babies, and sex, develop with age and maturity. It's important that their interest is responded to in an open and honest way. Children need the words for their body parts taught and explained in ways which help them cope. For example, it's no use teaching a five-year-old the word for penis, without being able to talk with him or her about the fact that class mates may call it a 'willy' and why different people have different words for the same thing. Such a discussion may well need to go on to deal with who should and shouldn't touch your penis and why we don't walk round with no pants on as the child may have done when younger. If such basic talk about bodies and sex is not a daily feature of children's lives then they will conclude that it is embarrassing, dirty, or unspeakable. Children need a vocabulary and information which frees them to talk about their bodies and sex. So, for example, saying to a three-year-old "pull your trousers up – don't be rude" introduces ambiguous and unhelpful concepts of disapproval about displayed genitals, when it would be more helpful to say "pull your trousers up or your bottom will get cold" or "you'll get a splinter in your bottom if you go on the slide" or "because that's what I do". The more openly parents can talk about bodies, the more likely it is that their children will have the confidence, vocabulary, and information to do likewise.

7. Parents adopting positive concepts of child sexual abuse prevention work with their children

One of the fears of parents is that they are unsure where to start in doing prevention work with their children. The above points outline that there is a huge amount parents can do to reduce the likelihood that their children will be assaulted and increase the chances the children will tell, if it should happen. A further way to help children talk about the problem, is to use the positive concepts in child sexual abuse prevention work in every day situations. The book "My Book My Body" provides a simple basis on which to build positive concepts about a child's body. They include: everybody has a body which is different; your body belongs to you; you have a choice about who touches your body; when people touch your body this can give you yes/no/don't know feelings; you should trust your feelings, and you should tell someone you trust about your feelings. Such an approach empowers children to believe in their own personal integrity and gives them the language and the permission to talk about situations or people who threaten that integrity. What such an approach doesn't do is dwell on the dangers that might happen to them and provide a basis for heightened fears and anxieties. One word of warning; children are infinitely resourceful in the way they can use our very best efforts to teach them, in ways which then thwart us as parents. We need to understand that this is what children will do and deal with their interpretations of what we have taught them with tolerance and good humour. One bouncy six-year-old said "It's my body, I own my body and I say what happens to it and I'm not eating those sprouts." We need to deal with these natural attempts to test out limits, in ways which do not undermine the overall message. So shouting or slapping a child to get the child to eat the sprouts is likely to undermine the message that she/he does own her own body; taking a good humoured but firm approach which says, "Okay, you chose if your body eats the sprouts and I'll chose if my body provides the pudding," is more likely to get the sprouts eaten and less likely to undermine the concepts.

8. Avoid making simplistic rules

When we are able to sit and think about the dangers that face our children, for example from traffic, it becomes obvious that there are no simple rules that will protect children. The steps we as adults take to protect our children from the dangers on the roads and help them understand the dangers and behave in ways which keep them safe, are extensive and complex; from buying special car seats, to teaching the green cross code, to supporting campaigns for speed humps, pelican crossings, etc.. We need to develop an equally extensive and complex range of strategies for keeping children safe from sexual assaults. Simple rules such as don't go to the park, don't talk to strangers, underestimate the problem and place the responsibility for avoiding danger on the child. There is little if anything a child can do but much we can do; such as supervising children closely, supervising other adults, being clear with schools about who should and should not collect our children from school, learning about the warning signs of abuse, campaigning for funding for prevention work and for resources to help children and families when abuse has happened. Simple rules don't solve difficult and complex problems.

9. When we have fears or concerns about an adult or a child we should discuss these with people we trust

Most of us can remember a person in our family or community, about whom we felt uneasy, or more than that, who made us feel unsafe or did things which were a sexual assault. We have all had experiences or memories of feeling scared or hurt and not being able to talk about it. One way for adults to reduce the number of children who will have those feelings in the future, is to be aware of the extent of child sexual abuse and be vigilant and alert to fears or concerns about an adult or a child. Some people deal with the problem of child sexual abuse by saying they don't want to know about it and trying to believe it won't happen to them and their families. The one thing mothers of abused children say is that it was the one thing they thought would never happen to them. Ignoring a problem doesn't make it disappear nor does it prevent it happening. If parents have fears or concerns about an adult or child however close, perhaps in the family, it's important to discuss these with people who they trust and who can help, such as Social Services, the Police, ChildLine, your child's teacher, your GP, or the NSPCC Child Protection Helpline, 0800 800500.

10. Believe your child if she/he says that she/he has been sexually assaulted

If children do lie about being sexually assaulted, it is almost always to say it hasn't happened when it has. Children are under enormous pressure not to tell about what has happened. Should your child or any other child tell you she/he has been sexually assaulted, the following would be helpful:

- Firstly, to say to the child "I believe what you are telling me."

- Secondly, to say that you are sorry that this has happened to the child.

- Thirdly, that what has happened is not the child's fault.

- Fourthly, that the person who did that to the child is completely responsible for what has happened.

- Fifthly, that in order to help the child and stop further abuse, what the child has said has to be passed on to people who can help.

Children who have been abused need, first and foremost, to be believed. One mother whose small daughter had been assaulted by her partner, wrote this poem to her.

When I was four
My world was safe
The monsters stayed in storybooks
My dreams evaporated with the dawn

When you were four
The monster roared
My worst nightmare was your reality

Thump Bump Thump

You run into my room
Eyes wide with fear
Body hot with sweat
And still I could not guess

But when you told
I saw the burden lifted from your shoulders
You walked to bed
Straight and tall
And slept a dreamless sleep
When you were four ......

Lucy

Your journey

When you hear about the abuse you are usually thrown into a turmoil of activity while you make sure your children are safe and the healing process begins. This is often followed by coping with your own grief and anger and helping your children come to terms with what's happened. As we have said earlier this often means helping your children through their disturbed behaviour. Hopefully after some time (and for everyone it's different, but usually after about a year) the signs that you have walked on are starting to show. It can then happen that the mother breathes a sigh of relief only to realise she is emotionally and physically completely drained. It happens to most mothers who have been through so much and have had to be so strong for so long.

Any mother's role is demanding. How many of us are allowed to let a thought enter our head and finish? We are usually interrupted by someone demanding something. A mother whose child(ren) have been sexually abused needs a lot more thinking time but is given less because of the demands made upon her. It is especially important at this time to get your needs met. We are not superwoman, we do not have a bottomless pit of loving and giving within ourselves which is never in need of replenishment. Chances are if you feel completely burnt out, it is probably because the intense pressure has gone and there is a breathing space. You are the most important person your child(ren) have. Treat yourself well. The strength you have to walk on with your family, shows you what you are and is a gift for your children. They will take your gift and be strong too, in time for their separate journeys. We wish you – mostly good weather, understanding, and peace of mind, as you walk on.

Useful reading

Brown H and Craft A, (1989), *Thinking the unthinkable*,
Papers on sexual abuse and people with learning difficulties,
FPA Education Unit, ISBN 0-903289-19-9

Byerly C M, *The Mother's Book: How to survive the incest of your child*,
Kendall/Hunt Publishing, Iowa, ISBN 0-8403-3640-3

Family Rights Group & NSPCC, *Child Protection Procedures: What they mean for your family*

Hooper C A, (1992), *Mothers surviving child sexual abuse*,
Routledge, ISBN 0-415-07188-7

Lambeth Women and Children's Health Project, *You and Your Child,*
A booklet for mothers of those who have been sexually abused.
(407 Wandsworth Road, London SW8 2JR)

NSPCC, *Child Abuse Investigations: A guide for children and young people*

Rouf K and Peake A, (1989), *My book my body*,
Children's Society, London, ISBN 0-907324-36-3

Russell D E H, (1989), *The secret trauma: incest in the lives of girls and women*,
Best Books, ISBN 0-465-07595-9